This is Where You Pivot

The Shift From Fear to Freedom

Elizabeth A. Miles

Ladybug Press

PHILADELPHIA, PA

Elizabeth A. Miles/ Ladybug Press
Thematic Editor, Copyeditor: Joshua Stuart
Cover Design: Elizabeth A. Miles

Book Layout © 2019 BookDesignTemplates.com

This is Where You Pivot: The Shift From Fear to Freedom/ Elizabeth A. Miles. -- 1st ed.
ISBN 978-1-7332829-0-1

To Norman, Jessica, Andrew, Abby, Mary, Maya, Brennan, Jake, Stacie, and Tanya: You have each contributed in some way to bringing this project to life. I can't thank you enough for your love, support, and encouragement. P.S. Thank you, Abs, for taking the concept for the cover art that was in my head and bringing it to paper, and for pushing me to finish the manuscript so that this book could come to life. You make the best cup of tea ever. P.P.S. Mary, I close my eyes and I can see (and hear) your beautiful voice singing and encouraging me along this journey. Thank you.

Deb, Al and Betty: You always told me there was a writer in me. Well, here she is! I hope I did you proud.

Josh: Thank you for your time in helping me flesh this story out. I am truly grateful.

To the Reader: Thank you for trusting me with a few hours of your time to read my story. I hope that these words inspire and encourage you, no matter where you are on your journey.

Contents

Introduction

THERE ARE MOMENTS IN LIFE when you must make a decision. Do you stay where you are—or move forward? It's not always an issue of choosing the easiest outcome. Sometimes you have to consider which option is best for you at the time, regardless of how easy it would be to choose differently or to walk away. Every day we are charged with making decisions that affect our lives. It can get complicated; even uncomfortable. At times it's downright painful. Those are the moments that can be toughest to push through, but they can be most rewarding at their conclusion. These are moments of growth—when we are pushed to move beyond what we perceive as our own limitations into something greater than we could have ever imagined.

This is where you pivot...

CHAPTER 1

Meeting the Mountain

I WAS STANDING NEXT TO A STREAM, in the middle of a central Pennsylvania campsite. It was a sunny but cool Wednesday afternoon. The site was set back a bit from a road that ran right through the campground. We set up our tent in an alcove just across from the stream. There was a fire pit and picnic tables right in the center. Winter had just turned to spring. Though not all of the leaves had come back, we were still well shaded by the tall maple trees that lined the site. For the next two nights my husband and I would be the only residents of this entire campground. The calm hush of the stream left a peaceful energy over us.

The inaudible words, *welcome home; this is where you pivot*, danced through the site, echoing off the stream and bouncing off the trees—all leading back to me. I had no idea where or who it was coming from or even what it meant, but I felt a tingling sensation over my entire body that left me with a serenity that I had never felt up to this point in my life.

Several weeks prior to arriving here my husband and I were separated, trying to work through some of the conflicts that had imposed themselves upon the relationship for years. The trip was a way for us to try to reconnect. A homecoming of sorts. Years ago, shortly after we had met, we went on a camping trip at a campground that looked very similar to this one. By the end of that weekend, we came home an engaged couple. Young. In love. Ready to conquer the world. In a way, it felt as though we had come full circle. There was a lot riding on this trip, at least that's how it felt.

As I thought back to that original trip so many years ago, connecting back to that young girl I was, *welcome home; this is where you pivot,* was still ringing through my mind.

The next day, during a hike in the mountains, the meaning of the message became clear.

At forty years old, I had only dabbled in light hiking in my life. And by dabbling, I mean it was more like gently strolling through the woods. On a paved path. With clear markers and a road that leads you from one end of the park to the next. Maybe a bench or two along the way to sit and rest. Little did I know, the hike I was about to embark upon was unlike anything I had ever experienced. It was exhilarating and a bit scary. That feeling you get when you know you've stepped outside of your comfort zone with no idea what the outcome will be. This time, I stepped so far outside of my own box, I knew I was not going to be able to live inside that same box ever again. Just a few months ago, I would have never allowed myself the opportunity to have this experience. My own self-doubt, fear, self-judgement, and overall lack of self-confidence would have prohibited me from saying "yes." But here I was, standing in a gorgeous state park, heading on a trek to see a waterfall. Little did I know that this would be the hike of a lifetime.

Upon arriving, we descended down a flight of stairs, arriving at a huge sign that read, "Hike at your own risk...sections of the trail ahead are steep and treacherous...hikers have been seriously injured and killed as a result of accidental falls from the trail and gorge overlooks...you are responsible for your safety." Freak-out city started happening in my mind. *Hang on*, I thought. *Why are there danger signs if we are just taking a walk in the park?*

I had let my husband do the planning for this trip. We knew we wanted to go camping and since he had always loved camping trips as a young scout and was familiar with the trails in our state (or so I thought), it seemed fitting that he would take care of the plans this time around. Up to this point, I was usually the one to plan the vacations, spending hours researching the best hotels, the best itineraries, trying to maximize the fun for our often-tight budget. Now, he was in the driver's seat. This was the one time in my life I let someone else plan a vacation, and here I was with absolutely no idea what I was getting myself into.

I looked at him and pointed back at the sign. I could feel my heart start to race. "Are you sure this is safe?" I asked him. The huge wooden park sign was providing enough evidence to the contrary.

My husband seemed so calm, cool, and collected. He looked at me with his warm blue eyes and rubbing his hand ever so gently on my back, answered, "We'll be fine. Don't worry about it." His voice was soothing and reassuring.

Everyone else at the trail that day seemed pretty relaxed as well. Yet the signs in front of us clearly said, in summary, "People have died trying this. Hike at your own risk." This to me translated to, "Hike this trail and *you, Elizabeth*...will...die!" Was I the only one who saw the sign? Was I the only one who cared?

Within a few steps of starting our adventure, we found ourselves at yet another trail marker that said, "This trail is extremely dangerous. Follow these rules to be safe: hiking boots only, no sneakers or flip-flops; No drugs or alcohol, stay on the trail, good physical condition of hiker required. People have been seriously hurt or killed by not following these rules."

With a nervous laugh I motioned to my feet and said, "thanks for insisting I get good hiking boots for this."

"No problem," my husband replied with a slight chuckle, seemingly without a care in the world.

I asked him one more time about our safety. He responded by wrapping his arms around my waist, pulling me in tightly towards him. In that moment, I could see the strong young man that I fell in love with so many years ago. He was only a few inches taller than me which made for the perfect embrace. It felt as though he would never let me go.

He gave me a quick kiss on the forehead and took a deep breath. "Do you trust me?" he asked.

That was the million-dollar question. Reluctantly, I answered, "yes, of course." The words came out of my mouth, but the rest of me screamed "no."

He motioned toward the trail. "Then let's get going. I'll keep you safe. What's the worst that can happen?"

Maybe I am reading a different warning sign, I thought. Or maybe I was just so scared my mind was playing tricks on me.

All I could do was point back to the sign, and with a deep breath tell myself, "I got this."

Initially, the hike didn't seem so bad. A little hilly. Some rocks. No big deal. That gave me a sense of confidence, and I started wondering what all the hype was about with the "danger" and "warning" signs. But as we continued to climb, the hike got steeper, rockier. A bit more challenging than that gentle romantic stroll I had envisioned for our trip. I expected picnic tables, barbecue pits, and lined, paved paths that clearly marked the beginning and end of the road. Soon, I realized I was climbing a mountain on what was essentially the edge of a cliff. *Oh! That* was what all of those danger signs were talking about.

I was not mentally prepared for this and scared out of my mind. There were points when I had to stop, take a breath, and calm myself down. I had to remind myself to shake off the fear. If I looked to my left, there was the cliff. If I made one wrong move, I would be a goner. Every so many feet, there were more "danger" signs. I was pretty sure that eventually the signs would start to say, "hey, idiot...why have you made it this far? Turn. Around." Looking up the path, I could catch a glimpse of the top of the waterfall. And I could hear the running of the water rushing down and crashing onto the rocks below. There was a sense of peace to the rhythm of the falls, and while I so desperately wanted the opportunity to see them, I didn't want to fall off the cliff trying to get there. "This is where you pivot" kept popping up in my mind. Like a flaming torch illuminating a dark cavern, this simple phrase provided light in one of my seemingly darkest moments.

So many other people were passing me on this trail. They were easily and calmly climbing this mountain. They all saw the same warning signs yet decided to do it anyway. Some of the people who passed also brought their dogs along for the walk. As I watched several four-legged friends so nimbly and happily climb the mountain with their people, I realized: this was more of a battle of my mind and body instead of a battle of me versus the mountain.

When we got to the half-way point to the waterfall, I sat down on a boulder to rest. My mind was racing and I felt like I was having an out-of-body experience. I saw myself on a television show. You know, that drama with the crazy mountain climbers, and everything goes completely and totally wrong and they need to be rescued. In that moment I felt as though everything was going completely and totally wrong, and *I* needed to be rescued. I kept screaming, "I can't do this. Make it stop!"

My husband packed a ham radio in his backpack. He told me he would have it with us in case of an emergency. "Can you call for help? I asked, with tears starting to run down my face. In my mind this was, in fact, an emergency—the only emergency he would ever need that radio for. I was shivering, perhaps in shock.

My heart was beating so fast that I thought it was about to jump out of my chest. I started to hyperventilate. I wanted my husband to tell someone, anyone, that he, too, was stuck on the side of this mountain with a woman who was having the panic attack of a lifetime. I envisioned a helicopter and a ladder dangling from the sky, and someone swooping in to lift me off the mountain and plant my feet back down on the ground at a normal (i.e. safe) level.

"If I called for help right now, they would tell us to do one of two things," he said, again with a voice so relaxed, strong, and certain. "Go back the way you came or get to the top and climb down the other side." I took a deep breath to calm myself. Again, he tried to reassure me. "I would not have brought you here if it wasn't safe. You can do this." He always knew how to calm me down in the middle of a crisis. "Right now," he said, his voice now more tense than before. "I need you to do me a favor."

"What's that?" I asked.

"I need you to calmly get up and stand against that tree over there and hold on."

I was confused. He had just told me I was safe, but in this second, I could sense something was wrong. "Okay...what's the matter?"

"I think I just felt the boulder shift. I think it's about to..."

I don't even know what the rest of that sentence was. I heard him say the boulder shifted, and I leaped off, grasping onto the roots of one of the trees sticking out from the side of the mountain. I was convinced I was about to die. *I hope my kids know how much I love them,* I thought.

But I had a choice to make. Fall apart on the mountain? Fall off the mountain because of my inability to see myself through this? Or get to the summit and find my way back?

Only three choices. All up to me to make the decision. Live or die.

Up until this point, I was begging my husband to make my fear stop. To put an end to my discomfort. I wanted to see the waterfall, but I didn't want to do the work that needed to be done to see it. All I had to do was stand up and climb the mountain in order to get to the top. Looking back, and re-reading that, it sounds so simple. But in that moment it was far from easy. I was so stuck in my own head. I didn't know what the next turn would bring. I didn't know what would be on the other side (or in this case, at the top). Or if I would even get that far to see it.

This is where you pivot.

That critical moment when you recognize that you have entered into a state of fear. You can stay on that path or choose to lean into the fear and climb over it.

The perfect metaphor for life. Each and every day we are climbing our own mountain, sometimes hitting an easy stride, while at other times it's a steep climb that we have to take on with all of our might. In those moments when life has us down, when all odds seem stacked against us, in our darkest hour, when there seems to be no hope, we can always choose the pivot.

How?

In the case of me vs. the mountain (or really me vs. my mind), I had to ask myself, "Why am I so afraid?"

Yes, it was a mountain. Yes, it was a cliff. Yes, I could have gotten hurt. But...every single day I make choices that could also expose me to hurt, pain, and suffering. So, why was this mountain going to get the best of me?

Self-doubt. Self-judgement. This climb was more about the thoughts and feelings racing inside of me rather than what was going on in the physical world. So, this my friends, is where we pivot.

Our Journey Begins...

HAVE YOU EVER CLIMBED A MOUNTAIN? If so, then you know that the ascent can offer perspective. Not just about the mountain, but life itself. One foot in front of the other, overcoming each new obstacle, step by step. It's a test of mental, physical, and emotional strength. When you reach the top, you might notice a new and refreshing point of view.

Pivot: "a shaft or pin on which something turns," "a turn or twist," "a central point or situation."

These definitions of the word "pivot" can all be applied to your life. Whatever the situation that is causing you to look and examine your life is the pivot. The actual decision of turning around is the pivot. And this situation is a central point in your life that will create change for your future self.

If you are reading along on this journey with me, first off, welcome and thank you for joining me. My guess is that you, too, have likely found yourself at a place in your life that has you looking for something else. Looking for more. Different. New. Maybe exciting. Have you been hiking or climbing a steep and scary mountain recently? Or just trying to get through your day-to-day life? Do you feel unclear or unsure of what the "newness" is that you are seeking? Or feel as though you are climbing through life and keep finding your way off the path? What will the view look like when you arrive at the summit? What is it like on the other side? Do you feel stuck? Alone? Afraid? So many questions to ponder. All important for our individual growth and survival. Keys to success. I've been there, too, friends, and continue to climb my own mountainous journey every day on a quest to something greater. We are on this journey together.

If you answered "yes" to any of the questions above, the emotions associated with that "yes" response is bound to replay in your mind. In one way or another, you will start to speak it until it manifests itself in the actions you take; over and over again. Enter the ugly self-fulfilled negative cycle of life that traps many of us. Without realizing it, it can have the power to shape who we become. And it plays right into emotions like guilt and shame. You want a different life. You know you *should* live better. Do better. Be better. But you've told yourself so many times that you can't. Maybe you feel that you deserve for the situation to stay as it is. You have convinced yourself that the mountain is too great a challenge to overcome, or that you are not worth pushing beyond the obstacle in front of you.

I know that we only just met, but please believe me when I say this...You deserve the BEST life possible. You deserve to be the best version of you. Whatever is going on for you on your mountain of life, *you* have the power to take control of the situation and live a life based on how you want to think, feel, and act.

Why the pivot? Why now? Because you are meant for greatness. You are capable of and are meant for more. Your life should be filled with an ease. A calmness. Not chaos. Do you believe that? Stop for a second and think about what you just read. What does that feel like? Do you believe it? Is it uncomfortable? Are you shaking your head thinking "she's crazy?" We're still pretty early on in our journey together, so I ask you to make a mental note of how you are feeling right now and then put aside any disbelief and continue through this with me.

Your days should be filled with joy and happiness. Anything that does not create joy in your life is sucking your time, energy, and resources. And where's the fun in that? We are here to live a purposeful, joyful life. Not live a life of chaos and drama. You are more than you have ever imagined, and it's time that you step into your greatness. And somewhere deep down inside, you know this. You feel it. You are craving it! But somewhere along the way, you got the message that it was not okay to acknowledge it.

It does not need to stay this way. The road to your freedom lies within you. You can climb your way to the top of your mountain, and then find your way to the other side.

Some might think, *Isn't it selfish for me to want more? Or to be more?*

In a word: NO! It's not selfish at all.

Tuning into to why you feel stuck and then taking the steps you need to move beyond that space is an act of self-love. Being true to yourself is an act of self-care. Consider this: there is a reason why they tell you to put your oxygen mask on first in the event of an emergency on an airplane. If you are taking care of you, then you are much-better equipped to help those around you. It allows you to nurture your best self, so that you can show up in your world in the best way possible for those around you, and for those who need you.

It is your right to live a life of happiness. It is your right to live in peace and calm. It is your right to live your truth—to acknowledge that you are here for a purpose and to live that purpose. You do not have to stay stuck. You have the power within you to change your situation. You have the power to choose a new life.

When you make the choice to take the path of least resistance in life, it does not mean that the obstacles go way. The climb does not stop. It just becomes easier and more enjoyable along the way. You can make the journey with a little more ease, stopping to enjoy the view as you progress.

If you don't believe any of this on the surface, there is a part of you deep down inside that knows this. That's why a book like this appeals to you. You are seeking the answers to the questions you keep asking...

How can I change my life? How do I create that success and fulfilment? Is it really possible? How do I get there? And who are you to tell me when and how and why to pivot?

Good questions. First off, yes, all of that is possible. And second, hello there! I'm Liz; now forty-years-old and have spent years worrying about my weight. Feeling stuck in my marriage.

Feeling stuck in my career. On a hamster wheel of control and judgement. I suffered with depression and anxiety. Food addiction. Chronic pain in my body. Two suicide attempts. Two inpatient visits to the psychiatric unit of the hospital. On the flip side, I am a mom of four, now a grandmother, and an entrepreneur. And through it all, both the good and the bad, things always seemed to feel a little out of place. I knew that I wanted more and believed in my heart and soul that somehow there had to be a way to turn my life around. I didn't quite understand how to get there. I read self-help books, watched inspirational and motivational videos online. Heck, I even had got a degree in psychology (and secretly felt that I could and should be able to psychologize myself better).

Ultimately, what I have come to realize is, no matter what situations are going on, there is always another choice, another path. Sometimes that path is covered with rubble, and is really hard to see, but it's there. When you are so focused on the problem or the path right in front of you, it is natural to feel stuck. You want a resolution to the issue presented. You want a way out. Sometimes you find yourself doing the same things over and over and over again, hoping for a different result. I know I did—for years. I thought I had to tackle each mountain head-on without acknowledging that there could be another, easier, simpler way.

This is where you pivot! And we have more of this mountain to climb. So, grab your favorite hot beverage or glass of iced tea, sit down and relax in your comfy spot, and let's begin.

CHAPTER 3

Base Camp

I WAS FIVE YEARS OLD, playing with my dolls on the front porch. It was a hot summer day in Philadelphia in the early 1980s. I was playing outside alone trying to get the water to stay in my doll's swimming pool. Across the street there were two kids from the neighborhood hanging out on the front step of a neighbor's house. I knew they were there but did my best to avoid looking in their direction; hoping that they didn't notice I was there. The two of them were so mean, bullying and teasing and mocking me every chance they could get. I didn't want to talk to them, and I tried my very best to stay out of their way as much as possible to avoid the torture. Sadly, the two of them eventually came over to my front porch, and started laughing and pointing at me, and telling me how fat and ugly I was. The typical bully banter. But then, one took it a little too far and told me to "watch out" because one day soon he was going to come over and "pop me with a safety pin, like a balloon." I didn't get angry. I didn't fight back.

I remember that day like it was a minute ago. I froze; shut down in complete and total fear.

In that minute, I truly thought I was going to die. This kid sounded so certain. I got the message loud and clear—I needed to hide. I drained the pool as fast as I could and packed up my dolls and accessories and headed inside. I wanted to tell on these kids, but I did not want to add "neighborhood snitch" to my already-long list of labels. At five years old, I was already known as the "ugly, dumb, and stupid kid," and the bullies on the block never wasted an opportunity to remind me just how low of a person I was.

In that minute, I stopped allowing myself to be myself. For the rest of that summer, and for the next three summers, I locked myself in my room with my six-inch black and white television, staring at reruns on the screen. I didn't go out to play anymore. There were no invitations to birthday parties. I remember listening to the other neighborhood kids playing outside, and I would watch from my bedroom window, wishing I could be down there, too. I wished someone would have called up to me and said "hey, come and play." But then I remembered that that kid was hunting me down, waiting to pop me like a balloon.

I looked different from all the other kids. I had a lisp and so I talked differently. I was taller than everyone else, including the boys, and I was a chubby kid. I was the natural target for being bullied, and bullied I was—terribly (as if there could ever be a not-so-terrible way of being bullied). Throughout most of first and second grade, I walked to and from school and on most days, the kids would find something to torment me about. My hair.

The way my knee-high socks wouldn't stay up at my knees. That tiny speck of lint on my school uniform. Over and over, I was told that I was fat, ugly, and stupid. There were a few kids who would be my friend when nobody was watching, but as soon as their friends were paying attention, they went back to preferring to be my enemy. It was hard to tell whom to trust.

I didn't know just how truly scared I was. And I didn't realize until much later just how closed off I became. I was not going to show people who I was. I was always trying to morph into whomever and whatever person I thought that the friendship crew of the day wanted me to be. I wanted to be part of the "in" crowd. I wanted to be "cool." I really wanted to be liked. I didn't know the secret recipe for "coolness," and truth be told, I was too afraid to trust anyone enough to open up. I spent recesses alone at my desk pretending to do homework or study when really I was hoping someone would notice me and come talk to me. When someone did come strike up a conversation, they usually just wanted to butter me up to get help (i.e. get answers) with homework. Rarely was it ever to really get to know me, or invite me to a party, or be my friend.

Fear and feeling as though I was not enough became the base issues that weaved their way through the rest of my childhood, and into my adolescent and adult years. It started when I was a young kid, so I got comfortable living in that state. I adapted, albeit not in the best of ways, but I figured out how to survive. I found ways to manage without it seeming that there were any problems at all. I decided that I was going to fit in one way or another, and I was adamant that I was going to decide what situations, conditions, and people were safest for me to be around.

Living in such a state of fear and control took me down a path of sadness, isolation, and depression. At sixteen, I found myself in therapy for the first time. That launched me into years of searching for more. Something bigger. Something better for my life. I continued in counseling for years. I sought out teachers who inspired me to believe that I could have a totally different life. I just didn't know how to get there. And then, eventually, I got sick and tired of feeling sick and tired. I was fed up with feeling low, sad, and depressed. Eventually, I had no choice but to make a change.

What I have finally come to understand is: I have one life to live. One chance, with a finite number of hours and minutes, to make something happen. So do you. It's a common thread that ties us all together. Because we are here with such little time available to us, we owe it to ourselves and to the world to create the best version of the life we want to live. Having that awareness is the pivot point from which anything and everything becomes possible. You, my friend, are a gifted and talented soul, with tremendous ability. The world needs your gifts. The world needs your light. You get to choose who you want to be—not for anyone else and not according to anyone else's rules or standards. Right now. In this instant. Not tomorrow. Not next week. Right now. What and who do you want to become? Step out of the box that others have created for you! Color and create the world that lights your soul on fire.

As a kid, it can be really challenging to understand that it's okay to be yourself. And I certainly did not understand how these events during my childhood were shaping my thoughts, beliefs, and behaviors at the time they were happening. There's so much pressure to be a kid who (_insert random list of accomplishments and labels here_), and many are quick to judge. For those of us who have lived our lives according to someone else's expectations, it's up to us to help the future generations see that they are capable of so many amazing and wonderful things. There is no box big enough to hold any of us back.

As we prepare to leave base camp, and move along in the journey, I encourage you to take a stroll down memory lane and think about those moments in your own life where you feel you were boxed in. How has it impacted where you are in life today? How has it shaped how you see the world? And how can you pivot?

CHAPTER 4

Icefall

IF YOU ARE CLIMBING MOUNT EVEREST, or have ever completed the trek, you will know the Khumbu Icefall. It's not far from base camp, but it can be the most treacherous part of the climb. Large, gaping crevices, falling pieces of glacier, and even an avalanche are all possible. Climbers accept this as part of their journey toward the summit. For the purposes of our story, our icefall takes place somewhere around adolescence. The time in our lives when just about anything and everything is bound to seem like an avalanche of emotion.

We fast forward a few years...

Now in seventh grade I was paired with one of the cutest boys in the class to work on a group project. Naturally, I had a crush on this kid, so this experience put me on anxiety overload. The project went on for about a month. Each week we had to finish a different piece of the project. So that meant regular contact with this boy, on a one-to-one basis. On the day the project was assigned, I didn't know if I should run, cry, laugh, or throw up. And the first time we worked on the assignment; my brain went to mush. I could barely remember my name, let alone write a sentence, and here this kid was sitting in my living room. There was no place for me to hide.

After we turned the project in, he continued to call me on the phone for a few weeks after. He just wanted to talk. Eventually, I got up the guts to ask him why he was still calling me. He told me he liked me, and he wanted me to be his girlfriend. OH! MY GOODNESS! I was seeing hearts and stars for days. Not only was he the cutest boy in the class, he was also considered one of the coolest. Part of the in-crowd. I felt like my social status had elevated by an exponential rate.

So here I was, the girlfriend of the cutest boy in school. Happy as a clam. Confused as all hell as to how that happened. Then, one day, I overheard a few of his friends talking at recess. They were talking about the fact that my new boyfriend was so happy that he had a new girlfriend, and her name was Elsie. My brain took a long, hard pause when I heard that. *Uh...excuse me?* I thought. There must be some mistake. I was his girlfriend. Who was this Elsie chick, and why did she think she was his girlfriend? On the next phone call, I got up the nerve to ask him about Elsie and he laughed.

"Elsie is nobody," he said. "It's L.C. That's you." At that point in my life the kids knew me as Liz. L.C. were the initials of my first and last name. When combined they sounded like "Elsie." He made up Elsie to cover up the fact that he was really talking about me. He was too embarrassed to let his friends know that he had a crush on me. He asked me to keep things quiet. He didn't want anyone to know.

My heart sank. I was crushed.

I thought I was being elevated to "cool girl" status. I felt so ashamed and humiliated.

Even as a teenager those days continued to haunt me. Though by that point when I was much more overweight I took on the mindset that I wished that first kid would have popped me like a balloon when I was five—deflating the weight that seemed to have appeared out of nowhere and was so hard to lose. Then people would love me. Yes, I had the cognition to understand that if he had tried to pop me, death likely would have ensued. But I didn't care. Parts of me had died that day anyway, and in that present moment as a teenager, there was a bigger part of me that wanted to die, which encouraged my first suicide attempt at the age of sixteen. Either way, my life would have had a very different outcome, and at that time I was so desperately looking for something else and wishing and praying so hard that I could live another life.

Perhaps you are thinking "those are just kids being kids" or "get over yourself—that's just what happens when you are young." As kids, we aren't able to comprehend or understand complex topics like judgement, vulnerability, shame, and fear. It's much more black and white. As a kid, we just conceive things as "good or bad," "right and wrong," or "hey, that horror movie scares me." Emotional abuse is a real-life issue that we rarely talk about, but the scars are long-lasting, and the wounds deep. As we grow up and start to forge a path for our lives, those deep-seated emotional scars are lingering there, unhealed. We don't even realize it. But these early experiences set the stage for our thoughts, feelings, and behaviors as we continue to learn, grow, and develop. By the time we get to adulthood we have accumulated a large number of these experiences, all culminating in us feeling unsettled about who we are as an individual, trying to mold and shape our bodies and our personalities to fit the mold and expectations of those around us. In a sense, as a child, we begin our hike through life on a relatively even path, that eventually starts to incline and get a little steeper. When we get older, our mountain can get complicated with lots of twists, turns, and detours along the way. The problem is that as kids and even as teenagers, our compass hasn't quite been calibrated yet, so it becomes easy to lose our way.

So how do you pivot out of, and away from, the unhealthy or the unintentionally misguided if your compass is on the fritz? On the mountain of life you need your intuition. Every one of us has intuition. That gut feeling that tells you something is good, or bad, or will bring you everything that you want in life.

Fear is the opposite of intuition. Fear is such a nasty four-letter word. I admit, fear is a mechanism that we all have in order to keep us safe. To make sure we don't die (to be blunt). However, most of the things we are afraid of will make us stronger. We are afraid to say what we really think or feel. We are afraid to take action on our dreams. Many of us are walking around right now living in fear. You want a different life and you don't know how to get started. But you are afraid to find out. Maybe you are afraid of success. Maybe you are afraid how your family will react once you achieve success. That can lead to anger. You feel stuck in a rut that you just don't know how to get out of. That anger leads to shame. You find yourself at twenty-five, or in your thirties or forties, or beyond, in a life that you didn't want for yourself, but you feel too stuck, angry, and lost to change. Maybe you feel ashamed because you feel like you are letting everyone down.

What is it that you want? What is your intuition telling you to do? Fear is going to tell you to do the opposite. Because in order to do that thing that you want to do, it's going to require change, action, progress, movement, which are all risky endeavors. And so, fear is going to convince you that your intuition is wrong, or bad, or is going to cause you harm in some way.

If you feel stuck, you need to move. One way or another. You need to choose another option. Action is the antidote to stuckness. Pivot, and make a motion towards another path.

CHAPTER 5

Camp 1: When Life Weighs You Down

IMAGINE A WORLD WHERE every day is cupcakes and brownies, cookies and whoopie pies. It's like heaven for any of us with a sweet tooth. And, boy, do I have a sweet tooth. There's something soul-satisfying to taking that first bite of the perfect fudgy brownie. Or dipping the fork into a huge piece of birthday cake. In the bakery every day is a celebration. It's your daughter's birthday. Your wedding anniversary. You got a promotion at work. Maybe you quit your job to start your own business. The bakery is the quintessential place of comfort. Not necessarily celebratory. Maybe you just got fired or laid off. Maybe you just filed for divorce. Food is a source of comfort and the bakery is the place where comfort lives.

The next stop on our mountain brings us into the bakeshop.

Habits are quick to form and difficult to break. My habit became food. Dessert, really. Anytime that I did a good job at school, I got a cookie. That made me feel love from my family. When I got married and we had reason to celebrate, there had to be a cake on the table. When my kids did something amazing, we celebrated with food. And the cycle continued on. On the flip side, if I was bored on a Saturday night I found comfort and friendship in a pint of ice cream. It tasted good. It became a habit that has taken me years to understand and attempt to change.

My relationship with food; and, oh boy, what a relationship; got pretty complicated around the time I was eight. Growing up in a food-obsessed family, I quickly got the message that there was always a reason to eat. And if you didn't clean your plate, it was a huge deal. Not only were you were disrespecting the chef, naturally (by grandma's standards), you were also going to die of starvation (also by grandma's standards).

At the same time, though, some of my best childhood memories involved food. When I was ten, my grandfather handed me a recipe for cinnamon raisin bread from a cookbook in his collection of many. When I gave it a go for the first time, I was in love. The dough was soft under my hands as I kneaded. I still remember that fantastic aroma of cinnamon and raisins in the dough. And, oh...my...word! How delectable the house smelled when a loaf of fresh bread was baking in the oven. And beyond the feeling of that soft, luscious dough between my fingers, and that spicy-sweet aroma from the cinnamon, I remember how much joy and pleasure the family got from eating that loaf of bread. The smiles of delight made the few hours of work in the kitchen well worth it. From that point on, I knew that whatever I did in life had to involve giving people that reaction. I wanted to bring joy to peoples' lives. I was going to be a chef, and comfort people by feeding them. At that age, it was as simple as that. "Food = happy" was a natural conclusion for me.

But with all the good also comes the bad. Let's face it—dessert is not a health food. Nobody eats cookies every single day to lose weight (oh, to dream the dream!). Once I discovered my love of baking, that lead me down a path of trying even more recipes. From very early on, I got the message that people would love me if I fed them. Having been pushed around at such an early age with kids who were pretty brutal while I was learning how great dessert could be, I was also learning that my body was something to be ashamed of. The more I was teased, the more ashamed I felt. The more shame I felt, the more food (sweets) I craved. And you can imagine how that turned out. I was heading into high school as the tallest, heaviest kid in my class. I didn't understand what feelings were or how to express them. I just felt as though nobody really liked me much, and I didn't like myself much either.

Through the up-and-down roller-coaster with weight, I kept disrespecting my body and my feelings. What I came to realize, eventually, is that I was numbing my feelings with food, and not paying attention to the body signals that I didn't want or need more food. That caused the weight gain. The problem then became the fact that I wanted to lose weight to look better to fit into what society told me I should look like. I equated "thin" with "people will like me" which caused so much anxiety and stress around body image and weight loss. I was always trying to live up to everyone's expectations of what they told me I should look like, so if I was ever able to lose any weight, it eventually came back. When that happened, I felt even worse for letting them down.

By the end of my freshman year of high school, I was bulimic. I couldn't figure out how to lose weight, and I just kept telling myself how much I loved food. So, I was going to eat it. But I knew it made me gain more weight. If I could find a way to prevent that, I'd be okay. I was desperately trying to take control of a situation that was beyond my control and understanding at that time. I felt gross. I felt shame. I felt sad. All the time. And I didn't know how to turn those feelings off in any other way.

After the birth of my second child, years later, I was able to lose 100 pounds with a diet of the good stuff (fruits and vegetables), and lots of exercise. I even found enjoyment in exercise. But babies three and four were soon born and life got even more hectic. With four kids, working full-time, and a rocky marriage, taking care of my body took a back seat to every other thing happening in my life. Through the tears of sadness and joy, my old friend dessert was always there. And so, the weight came back, and then some, and at the age of thirty-six, I found myself weighing almost 400 pounds and feeling worse than ever—about the number on the scale, about my body, and about where I was in life. I was an overachiever who wanted to make sure everyone saw that I could handle any obstacle life threw at me. No matter how bad I felt on the inside, all everyone was ever going to see was that I was okay.

Eventually, I started to make the connections between those moments when I would slip off of my diet plan and my feelings in those moments. Ironically, those were the same moments that triggered the same kind of panicked reaction when faced with the possibility of slipping off the side of the cliff. I just didn't whine and scream and cry about them like I did while hiking. Instead, I used the food to stuff the anxiety and fear down further.

Pinpointing exactly where and when things went wrong allowed me to connect the triggers to my behavior, which gave me the clarity I need to make adjustments.—to pivot. One day, I was working in my bakeshop and felt way behind the 8-ball trying to ice a cake and get ready for that night's event. I felt pressure. I felt anxiety. I felt like time was running out. Suddenly, just like that (finger snap), I grabbed a brownie and went to town. Suddenly, the diet didn't matter. My health didn't matter. My weight-loss goals didn't matter. Nothing else mattered but the moment I was sharing with that brownie. It was a downward spiral that I saw coming. I could have bet money on it. In reality, I was trying to eat my way out of the anxiety.

I still had to run some errands before the event began. By the time I got back to my store, I had just enough time to shovel some food into my mouth. I had gone all day without really eating a solid meal (brownies don't count). I waited all that time. And because I was so hungry at that point, I never really got to taste the food. I couldn't even tell you what it was that I had bought for myself. I was so hungry and didn't care by that point. I felt that I had so little time before the event, so I hurried myself through the meal. Feeling so rushed, I never gave myself the breathing space to think before taking another bite. The spiral was inevitable.

There were so many reasons to lose weight, it seemed. In reality, there was only one real, powerful reason why. Part of my path became figuring out what that "why" actually was. I knew what behaviors would lead to the change, but I couldn't bring myself to do them. The "why" was there, I just couldn't see it yet. There were a ton of reasons for me to change. But only one reason keeping me from actually making any improvements or accomplishments. I couldn't get out of my own head.

I would start a diet and on day one I would think to myself, *What the heck did I just do? I own a bakery. I've identified as a baker for my entire life.* The dream of owning my own shop has been in my head since I was eight. How could I give up dessert? Dessert had been my friend for... well, forever. How could I break up with it now? We had been so good together. And what would everyone else think when they hear of this journey? Will they say? "There's the fraud baker who gave up dessert." "Her cookies must not taste good—she doesn't eat them herself." And what the heck would I do now when I was bored? Cranky? Sad? Lonely? Or when we needed to celebrate at home? And what if...I failed?

One brownie led to a cookie. That led to a cinnamon roll. Eek. In the days right after, I felt so angry with myself, and a bit hopeless. I believed that I would never be able to regain composure or control over the situation. At the time, I didn't understand that even the simple act of seeing the program was me regaining composure and taking control. I saw the problem. And was working on the solution. Nobody could do it for me. There was no super hero flying in to make this right. I was (and am) 100% responsible for this. I had to do it for myself. That's the only way out. I needed to put one foot in front of the other. Even if I had to go crawling. I needed to be the one to do the work. Just like on the mountain.

Why did I care so much about losing weight? Because I knew that I have an addiction to food. Because I recognized that unhealthy eating was not serving me in my life. Because I understood that this cycle was contributing to illness, pain, and feeling like I am a big disappointment. Because looking in the mirror, I saw someone who has failed time after time. And that wasn't really working for me anymore. At the time I was two years into my business. Looking away from the mirror, I saw and still see successes and victories that I could have never imagined. But I always had to come back to looking in the mirror, still not liking what I saw. As great as those business and family wins were, this battle with food is something that I needed to overcome if I was going to take things to the next level in my life.

I was so concerned about the judgement from other people, and that kept me down for a long time. I felt so bad that other people were looking at me and thinking "look at that fat girl" or when they would see me and my husband together would think "poor him, he could have done so much better." There were times that I would be out on a date night with my husband; if a girl walked past us, I would assume he would be more attracted to her than to me, because, well, I knew what I looked like in the mirror. The truth is, I was judging myself and the world harder than anyone else could have been judging me, and I wasn't giving my husband any credit that had he not been attracted to me he would not have said "yes" when I asked him to marry me.

I took that fear of judgement and allowed it to keep me down. Instead of taking it and saying, "screw the world—I am going to lose this weight and look amazing, and feel amazing," I used what was going on in my head as a reason to stay exactly where I was—stuck, overweight, and feeling like crap in my body and about my body.

It's easy to say, "who cares what people think," but the reality is—we all care what other people think of us. As humans, we all want to be liked and loved by other people. We are social creatures; we want to be accepted by society. Eventually I realized that how other people might like or love me, and how I love myself are different. I need to look myself in the mirror and be proud of and happy with who I am. And it's not (totally) about the number on the scale or the size of my pants. It's very much about how I feel inside my own skin, and whether or not I have energy to take on all that I want to accomplish in life. It's about whether or not I can love myself enough to take time out of life to do the things that make me happy. That's the pivot point. The place where we choose something beyond whatever it is that gets us caught in the crazy chaos of whatever is happening in the world. Choose yourself. Choose happy—whatever that looks like for you!

Key words there: do the things that make *you* happy!

For a few years, my vision board showed the vision of losing 150 pounds, no longer needing medication for diabetes, and no longer feeling so much physical pain in my body. Each year, I wanted to make it *the* year of loving myself so much that I would lose the weight. I knew there was a connection between self-love and what I thought about my body, and how my body looked. I did part of the work. I meditated. I journaled. I hit the gym at 5 a.m. I did "most" things right...for about three weeks. And then those actions died out. I thought that the one thing stopping me from reaching this goal was the one thing that I have known my entire life, and the one thing that came to be my identity—food. I understood that my relationship with the cupcake needed to change. My actions had to be big and powerful. It couldn't just be a half-assed attempt. This had to stick.

One day I had a thought. What if I went without dessert for a whole month? Immediately, irrational thoughts popped into my head. Would the world stop turning? Would life as I knew it end? Would people think I was a fraud? What happens when a baker and self-proclaimed foodie sets out on a journey of thirty days with no dessert? What happens when the Band-Aid comes off, and you force yourself to find comfort in places other than the refrigerator?

For my entire life, the word "diet" brought thoughts of complete and utter dread. To me, it meant strict food regimens, discipline, and restriction. It meant avoiding the foods I want to eat. I didn't like any of those things. I started referring to diets as "projects" instead. By calling it a project makes it a completely different vibe. Project inferred choice. I was simply choosing to not eat dessert. It's not a diet. It's a project. And given what I have told you about me so far, you might have guessed that I am good at projects. I ace projects. Nothing less than 100%. Essentially, I was trying to outsmart myself with semantics. Whatever worked, right?

Looking back now, it was not just about the food. The food was an external symbol of what was going on inside. It wasn't just my relationship with food that needed to change. If I didn't look within myself, food could have been replaced with any number of other things. I wasn't focused on my feelings. I wasn't focusing on self-care and self-love, or valuing who I was as a person, or identifying as someone who could create something of value in the world.

This is where you pivot.

Health is so much more than the number on the scale, or the size of your pants. It's also about having energy to do the things that make you happy or that life requires of you on a daily basis. It's about being at peace with your body no matter its shape, managing stress, and giving yourself some love on a regular basis. What you see in magazines or on television or in movies; those are stories and images created by someone else. Made-up characters and settings. Not your life. Do not judge yourself or your self-worth based on someone else's story, setting or cast of characters.

With regards to food, relationships, and self-care the pivot comes the minute we choose another path. Every time we make a different choice and every time we ask that all-important question "why" we are choosing to pivot. It will create change in your life. You don't have to stay stuck in the crazy. You have the power to create any change you want in your life. You deserve it.

Another quick note: It's important to pause and recognize that there is tremendous benefit in understanding that we find some sort of value in staying stuck in the position we are in today. Let me repeat that, because it's important. Wherever you are in your life right now, even if it's not as nice of a picture that you say you'd like for yourself, you are getting some sort of benefit from it. My weight became part of my story. It gave me a barrier of protection. The world was a scary, cruel place for me, so I hid behind my weight. As long as I had that weight the world would never see the real me. At the time, that was okay. I was protected from the judgement and all of the negativity that I felt from the world around me. People didn't expect much from me because I never allowed myself to show up fully and presently. I worked hard, don't get me wrong. In the jobs I held, I always aimed high. I talked a great game. I wanted to advance and always worked hard enough to move up in position. But just when it got to the point where I was about to rank up, so to speak, I would find some fault in the position or the company, or I'd make some major mistake that would cause me some issues. I was sabotaging myself big-time. I didn't want people to know exactly what I was capable of. Honestly, I wasn't quite sure what that looked like either, but I knew it had to be more than what I was giving at the time. I wasn't willing to open up to the world. The weight stayed on and continued to protect me through all of those times when I chose to hide from the fear.

I found myself depressed, sad, scared. I was also diagnosed with fibromyalgia. I was in so much pain, physically, mentally, and emotionally. The physical symptoms were easy to understand. Doctors told me to eat more salad, less cake, and exercise more. And they kept prescribing more and more medication, only a few of which actually did much to prevent symptoms, and

most had a host of side effects, namely and most problemati-
cally, weight gain. Many of the medications interacted with
others that I was taking, so the doctors continued to prescribe
more and more to counteract side-effects. I was a walking phar-
macy and felt like a zombie. There had to be a better way.

The pivot happened for me when I realized I could take control of my life. Rather, that is when the first pivot occurred—
when I really and truly understood that I was here for a greater
purpose. I had always sensed it in years past, but there was so
much junk piled on top of it, and it took me a while until I realized that I deserved it...that it wasn't just a wish or a pipe
dream...that it was actually possible. I began to understand that
in order for me to achieve all that I wanted to achieve in life, I
would need to face the fears. I would need to face the world. And
show up. Once I recognized this fact, I had to choose to either
surrender to the fear or continue to hide away.

I wasn't sure which option was scarier. I didn't care. I just
didn't want to stay feeling stuck and powerless anymore.

CHAPTER 6

Camp 2: Awareness + Action = An Easier Climb

AT FORTY YEARS OLD I WAS overweight, still battling with my weight, and battling the demons in my own mind. At the time that I was hiking the mountain, I was also trying to bring my marriage back together. I couldn't ignore the fact that part of me was worried that if I didn't make it up that mountain my husband would think poorly of me. Looking back, I realize that there was a part of me thinking that everyone who passed me was saying, "oh look at her, thinking she can climb a mountain." Or they would look at me standing beside my husband and recognize how much of a basket case I was and think, "oh, that poor guy is stuck with her."

Three weeks prior to the mountain climbing trip, on a random Monday afternoon, I found myself standing in the middle of another local state park. It was a cool, sunny day in March. There and then I realized for the very first time that I was a grown up. And for the first time, I truly understood what that meant. As a kid I always thought that "being a grown up" meant getting married, having kids, buying a house, graduating from college, going to work every day. Period. End of story. I equated "growing up" with the stuff that comes along with it. I thought it was more about the actions that take place during that phase of one's life, and less about the maturity, thoughts, and feelings that come along with the territory.

In terms of the stuff—the actions—of being grown up, I had what I thought was the recipe of a successful grown-up-hood...

- I started working at the age of fifteen.
- I went to college.
- I met the love of my life at the age of nineteen. At the age of twenty, we were married.
- At twenty-one, I gave birth to my first child and within two weeks after her birth we closed on our first home.
- I got a job quickly out of college.

So, as far as my original, albeit limited, definition of being a grown up went I was making money, married, and had kids. I was CRUSHING it and checking off all the right boxes of my so-called grown-up life.

Then why did it take me so long to truly become a grown up? Because, in reality, back when I was twenty, I was sucking at it. I was getting up every day and going through the motions, completing tasks that I thought were necessary to be happy and successful. The key word there: *thought*. I was living a life that someone else told me I needed to have, defining "adulthood" based on a set of actions that someone else decided. And trying to make myself feel emotions that I thought were supposed to come with the territory.

As a kid, going to college was never a question. It was a requirement. I was constantly told to choose a career that would bring me the most money. I had to find a husband who would take care of me because, as a woman, I wouldn't be able to take care of myself. And I had to have kids. But nobody ever stopped to teach me about fulfillment, or purpose, or living my joy. Or managing emotions. There was no talk about what true love is or what it means to be a mother or wife. I had to figure all of that out on my own.

A little backstory from that day my husband and I were hiked on the side of that dangerous mountain...

I went to Fort Washington State Park for my version of hike (a gentle stroll on a paved path) with my husband. We had just finished our hike and were talking about our relationship and what we each hoped to see happen (reconciliation). The sun was shining. The birds were singing. And there was peace. Not because I wasn't still upset and hurt and angry with my husband, but because I could still find peace and calm in the midst of that pain. And...I recognized that he was also experiencing pain and sadness and hurt and anger. While we love(d) each other and wanted to be together, it was our childish behavior and lack of emotional maturity that drove us apart.

For twenty years we acted like selfish toddlers in big people bodies. We looked grown up. We sounded grown up. We played the part of a grown up so well that it fooled everyone around us (even ourselves). In reality, we had no self-awareness. No control over our minds, hearts, or actions. No connection between actions, emotions, circumstances. No understanding of why we acted as we did. Just action, reaction, repeat. It was a roller coaster of emotion, full of confusion, anger, love, hate, lots of yelling, and more tears than I could ever count.

Ironically, about two years prior to this day in the park, I started on a mindfulness journey. I started learning about self-love, affirmations, and mindset. I was able to apply it in some situations, but not all. I was going through the motions, so to speak. I thought I could simply "mindset" my problems away. Wake up, say my affirmations, and the world around me would somehow change. I would wake up to the life that I wanted. At that time, I didn't understand why things weren't working—for me, for my marriage, for my career, for my family. Still, I was going through the motions, checking off the boxes, but not actually making the changes.

Then I realized—there are no results without action (yes, I had heard that statement in the past, but never actually understood it). The Universe will help you through, as long as you are open to receive the guidance but there is still work to be done to see results. Part of that work involves looking at your own "stuff" and cultivating your ability to understand emotions, thoughts, feelings, and triggers. You have to look back at what has happened in your life to understand your actions in the present, and then have compassion and understanding for what others are going through, recognizing that it isn't "all about me."

A month before that hike, I hit what I consider to be one of many rock bottoms in my life. This one seems to stick out as a pretty major and defining moment in my life. My husband left. My daughter gave birth to my first grandbaby, and the labor and delivery were incredibly rough. I got news on my business that was not so fun to hear. So, basically in a span of a few months I lost my love, I almost lost my daughter and grand baby, I was about to lose my business, and to top it all off I was having some medical issues. Emotionally and physically I was completely and utterly exhausted. It seemed like things could not have gotten any worse.

I should mention that my husband had left several times before, but this time something about his leaving felt different. And I was ready for it to be so.

Growing up, I was the hopeless romantic. I believed in fairy tales and love at first sight. Because of that I went into romantic relationships with the expectation that my boyfriend would treat me like a princess. I believed in old-school chivalry—with the guy opening and holding doors, paying for the date, and saying something romantic and sweet to make me feel good. I envisioned candlelit dinners, moonlit carriage rides, and being showered with roses and sweet messages on my voicemail or by text.

That is not at all how dating went for me. I started dating when I was sixteen. Steve was his name. Good old Steve. Everyone thought he was such a great guy. Smart. Funny. Kind of a wise-ass. He paid attention to me and said just enough of the right things to make me feel a sense of security. It never occurred to me to question why he was so reluctant to hang out with me, or why he would constantly give me reasons why he couldn't go out. Until I discovered he was also seeing two other girls at the same time.

Then at seventeen, I met Mike. Good old Mike. Everyone thought he was such a great guy. Smart. Funny. Kind of a wise-ass. He paid attention to me and said just enough of the right things to make me feel a sense of security. I couldn't question why Mike was reluctant to hang out because he was a little bit older than me, and was usually away at college, so there weren't many opportunities to see one another. But then I discovered he had slept with, and was dating, a girl who lived down the hall in his dorm.

The cycle continued. Then I met the man I married. Everyone thought he was such a great guy. Smart. Funny. Kind of a wise-ass. He paid attention to me and said just enough of the right things to make me feel a sense of security. I was convinced he was the right guy for me. Within a month of us meeting and dating, we were engaged. The ask wasn't all that romantic, nor was the "yes." We were on a camping trip sitting by the fire. I turned to him and said, "I love you—marry me," to which he replied, "I am not sure." Later that evening he caved and said "okay." While his reluctance was a red flag, I never questioned it further. Then a few months later, in the middle of planning flowers, location, and coordinating bridesmaids, I discovered he was having an affair with multiple women at the same time.

You aren't having déjà vu. And you haven't been re-reading the same part of the story over and over. And the publisher didn't print the same paragraph multiple times. The same story repeated over and over in my life for years, and even into my marriage. Once I found out about his affairs (pre-marriage), I initially called off the wedding. Then a few days later, I convinced myself that it didn't feel right to call it off. Something about the situation did not feel right at all. In reality, what wasn't right was the way I was being treated, but I believed that the wrong part was calling off the wedding. The hopeless romantic in me believed that because he said he was sorry he would treat me better from then on, and we'd live happily ever after.

Boy, was I wrong—dead wrong.

That cycle continued for years. He would cheat. I would scream and yell and cry. He would say he was sorry and would never do it again. I would take him back. Through the years, the situation got more and more complicated as we added kids to the equation, a house, and more good memories mixed with the bad. Every time I believed that I was the reason he cheated. It was all my fault. I was too fat. Too ugly. Too stupid. These were the reasons (in my mind) that I was not being a good wife. I convinced myself that if I worked a little harder at making things perfect at home—and for me that meant things like making him the perfect dinners, making sure we had plenty of family time, and not getting on him about things like the lawn being mowed, or the house needing to be tended to—then he would love me and everything would be okay. And he would forget about the women he was with. He would come clean to them and tell them he was happily married to the most wonderful wife in the world.

That. Didn't. Happen.

Instead, he continued to lie. Continued to come up with bigger stories about why I was the evil queen of the house. Continued to make himself out to be both a hero and a victim. And the women he saw at the time all believed him. One of the biggest knives to my heart came when I realized that there were these women out there thinking I was this monster of a person and had no idea they were the ones sleeping with the real monster. I wanted to prove him wrong, and worse, I felt I needed to prove myself to these women whom I would never meet, and, in reality, didn't matter much at all to my life outside of the marriage situation.

This man who had committed himself to me in front of our family and friends, who promised to love, honor, and cherish me all the days of our lives, had torn me apart emotionally. I hated it, yet I allowed it. Eventually, I came to realize that I was allowing him to bully me around, just as I had allowed my peers to bully me around as a kid. I didn't know how to make it stop. I could have kicked him out. There were times that I did. And then the fear kicked in. I started to regret that choice and would beg him to come back.

Fast forward about twenty years to that day my husband left, yet again; I was the worst possible version of myself that I could ever be. Cold. Harsh. Mean. Completely irrational. Telling him to go and wanting him to fight me on it. Pushing him away while secretly hoping that he would take me in his arms, look me in the eyes, and profess his unending love for me. I was reacting to situations that could have been discussed calmly, but because things were not going my way, and I didn't know how to express my true feelings, the conversation instead turned into a scream-ing match. It came as a surprise that, when I told him to leave, he packed his stuff and went. This had happened before. And on each occasion, I was crushed. I would sit there thinking *how could he leave me?* And *what was wrong with me?* I was truly shocked in those moments that he left, even though he did exactly what I was telling him to do. Saying that I was confused and heartbro-ken barely scratch the surface to how I was feeling inside. By him packing up and leaving, in my mind he was proving he never loved me in the first place, and reinforced that I was not worth the fight. And that felt awful. In reality, everything was wrong—how I defined my life, how I saw myself, how I thought others saw me. The value of other people's opinions took such a high priority that I missed sight of the fact that I needed to have a high value of myself.

I recognize now that his behavior was wrong on so many lev-els. Manipulative. Deceptive. I was his doormat. I was his backup plan for when the women he was seeing on the side decided they didn't want him anymore or gave him less attention than he wanted from them. I didn't believe there could be another way. I had given up so much of my own power to this situation that I didn't see any other possibilities, and I believed on some level that I truly deserved this pain. This was all there was for me. I was not worthy of any better.

I was missing out on some really sweet stuff in life. Like peace and calm. Laughter. Fun. Playtime. Self-discovery. At one point, I started to lose my belief in fairytales and romance. I was walk-ing around not feeling worthy enough to pursue any goal or dream that came to mind. Who was I to (insert any big dream here)? That was the story I continued to tell myself.

"I Think I Can" and Climbing Past Self-Limiting Beliefs

MAHATMA GANDHI SAID: "Your beliefs become your thoughts, your thoughts become your words, your words become your actions, your actions become your habits, your habits become your values, your values become your destiny."

Phew...that's a lot. And it's absolutely true.

I believed that I was not enough and not worthy of love, success, or happiness. I believed that I deserved to be treated with such total and utter disrespect that I continued to be married to a man who valued himself and his own need for power, control, secrets, and manipulation, so much so that it came at the expense of my own self-worth, my own mental health, and the mental health of our kids.

But back to Gandhi's quote. Think about it for a minute. Whatever it is that you believe to be true is what you are going to think about. In this case I am referring to all of those hurtful things we tell ourselves. Things like:

- "I'm ugly."
- "I am fat."
- "I am a bad mom."
- "I am poor."
- "I will never amount to anything."

If you buy into any self-limiting belief it will replay in your mind like a broken record. And one way or another, you will start to speak it. Until eventually you start acting like it. It's a nasty cycle that leaves us feeling bad, guilty, even shameful. There are expectations put upon us, by someone else, and when we don't feel as though we are "living up," we start to feel guilty. Eventually fear sets in and we begin to believe that we can't do any better, and don't deserve to try.

How did this happen?

There were a lot of little punks running around my neighborhood treating me like I was a piece of garbage. That was strike one for me. Not to sound cliché, but a big part of it came from my parents, the environment in which I was raised, and the early experiences that I had as a child. Somewhere very early on in life, many of us get the memo that life has to be hard. That control is required in order to achieve anything and everything that is desired. That money is hard to come by. That the status or situation we start out with has to remain the status or situation we stay in.

Maybe this sounds familiar to you. I grew up with an interesting recipe for a chaotic life.

I observed my parents who were constantly fighting. On one side of the boxing ring was my mother who tried to control everyone and everything, and basically buried herself in her work to avoid her problems in her marriage. On the other side of the ring was my father who worked two jobs to put food on the table, cheated on my mother, was verbally abusive, and ended up turning to drugs to relieve his own pain.

My grandfather lived with us when I was growing up. He ended up becoming more of a parent than a grandparent. He was there every day when I got home from school. He made dinner for us every night. Sometimes he would drive me to events or to my friends' houses. He was a mother figure, as well as a father figure, to me and my brothers. But he, too, contributed to the comments and mocking when it came to matters of my weight.

Being overweight as a kid, as well as the tallest and first to develop in the grade, the kids in the neighborhood never missed the opportunity to tease, mock, and ridicule how I looked. And by the way, I was smart, too, so I got teased even more for having good grades.

I watched my parents constantly struggle with money. There was always just enough, but never more. They worked hard, so I believed that I needed to work hard, too. In school, I believed that my worth was set by the grades I got in school. That I was only worth loving if I got an "A" on the test. That set me out on a quest to never fail. As an adult there were points when I believed that my worth was set by my job title. I always had to be the first one done on any project, and I had to have done the best job, hands-down over anyone. I believed that overachievement would put me on the path to success in life. I also felt a tinge of pain and resentment when those around me received accolades for doing a good job too.

The results of that childhood and early adulthood? I continued to be overweight for most of my life. I grew up feeling ashamed and scared. As a result of my own insecurities about myself, I led myself down a rabbit hole of control. I based my success on other people's opinions. I thought that success meant having a fancy job title. I tried to direct the opinions and thoughts of others so that they would yield to me and my will. I wasn't truly acting as a good friend, a good wife, or a good person. I wanted to be seen as one, but my intentions were pretty self-serving. Later in life I came to recognize that I was living with the limited belief that anyone who tells you they love you will eventually let you down, so I continued to create a situation that gave me control over who came and went in my life to avoid the pain of that letdown.

I never really felt a strong connection with my parents, and while I so longed for a strong connection with my kids, I couldn't see that I was struggling so much with my own issues that I was preventing that from happening.

My poor relationship with my parents, and my lack of self-worth and self-love left me directionless as a teenager and young adult. I had no idea what I was going to do with my life. In school, I put a lot of pressure on myself to work hard and never settle for less than an "A." When projects were assigned, I started them the day they were given, even if I had six weeks to do them. I completed them in two. Homework was done as soon as I got home from school. If ten math problems were assigned, I would do fifteen. I wanted to impress the teacher. I never wanted to get in trouble in school. Homework was done. Always. I did what the teacher said. Never questioned anyone or anything. The people around me kept telling me to "go where the money was," which really just taught me that I needed to trade time for money. There was no "follow your heart" when I was a kid. No "follow your passion." And besides, I was too busy doing homework and making everyone around me love or like me that I didn't have much time to figure out what I was even passionate about.

That lead me to not really knowing what I wanted to do when I grew up. I had straight "A"s. Decent enough SAT scores. I was involved in activities. On paper, I had it together, but, in reality, I was directionless. As a grown up, I continued to search long and hard for the "dream job." For the fast track to success. Skipping from job to job searching for the one that would put food on the table and fulfill my every need and desire. As soon as I had any thought or idea of which direction to take, fear would set in and I would feel too afraid to do anything. The path of becoming a pastry chef, and even entrepreneurship, were not highly favored when I was a kid. There were no You Tube channels for chefs, no cable TV channels devoted to cooking and baking. I wanted to be a CEO. Didn't matter where or doing what.

I knew I wanted to be a wife and a mom and I wanted to have it all—a great house, family, and a high-paying job. I pushed myself to work so hard—for my peers, kids, and husband—because I couldn't let anyone down. But I ended up mostly letting myself down. I was constantly finding more and more things that were wrong with me. I was "bad" and "broken." These ideas played on repeat throughout my entire life.

I had heard the term "surrender" in the past. And I thought I was doing a good job of it. But I was missing the mark. And then, one day—that all changed.

This is where you pivot.

We often think of "surrender" as a bad thing. You "surrender" to the law. We know that when someone "surrenders" they have given up in battle. But surrendering has nothing to do with punishment, defeat, or even failure. When we surrender to life, we become accountable for our own actions, thoughts, and decisions while recognizing that there are things outside of your control. The surrender is important. It helps you let go of the things that are holding you back from living the life you want and deserve.

Your mind tries to control everything. In reality, your mind is trying to protect you. We try to avoid pain and gravitate toward (or push for) all things pleasurable in life. It's a constant struggle. You will continue to try to change the things, people, places, and circumstances that you do not want in your life. Eventually, there will come an instance that you cannot continue to fight. Good, bad, or ugly, it's powerful! This is when you surrender. You recognize that you have tried everything you can, and none of those strategies have brought you to the place you desire. You don't know what to do anymore. You have a vision for your life, but don't know how to get there. When you surrender, you don't know what's going to happen next. It might be good. It might be bad. But it will be different. The surrender occurs when you recognize that your current circumstances are not working for you and can no longer continue for you.

Wait a minute. Isn't that the same thing as giving up? Eh...not in the way you might think. You aren't giving up on the situation. You are giving up the idea that you can or should control it in any way. You give yourself a much-needed breath of fresh air (not to mention peace and calm) in your life just by recognizing that your actions up to this point have not worked. You recognize that maybe you have done everything the right way so far, but the goal has not been achieved.

Separate the action(s) from the outcome. The real goal is to be present, and you do so by asking yourself: "How do I feel in this moment?" That is what really matters.

There were points when I thought I had surrendered. I said it. "I surrender." I thought I felt it. But the real surrender for me happened the day that my husband and I separated. Again.

I had to look at life a little deeper. Twenty years together and none of it was easy. He would cheat, I would find out, he would promise to never do it again, and I would take him back. This cycle continued for too many years of our marriage.

I didn't trust myself enough to stand up for myself or for what I deserved in a relationship. I wasn't trusting my intuition. Deep down I also didn't believe I was worthy of any better.

Why did I stay? It all boiled down to one word: fear. Fear of failure, fear of what my parents would think, and fear of not being good enough. In fact, I felt a lot of things. Anger. Sadness. Hopelessness. Rejection. But I didn't have anyone around me at the time that could help. Sure, there were plenty of people around me. My family was local. But I wouldn't let them see the full depth of what was happening. They saw what was happening on the outside, yet I was too scared that if anyone saw what was really going on inside of me that they, too, would run screaming. It was the same type of fear that came up every time I caught my husband in another lie or affair.

Eventually, there came a point in the marriage when I had a real surrender moment. Things were falling apart. I felt so helpless and hopeless. We were tearing each other apart on a rollercoaster of love-hate. I recognized that I couldn't do anything in that moment other than simply stop. I had the choice. I could continue fighting. I could continue feeling bad. I could continue riding on the hamster wheel.

That's what I had done for so long and had gotten me nowhere. I had to let go. I had to surrender.

This is where you pivot.

I recognize that my husband went through some pretty awful stuff as a kid and saw some pretty nasty things in his early adult life. Despite the good times (and the bad), I knew that he was suffering. And, perhaps this is the case for you, too. We all go through stuff. It's part of life. But we are given a choice—you can let those things keep you down, or you can view those experiences as lessons and opportunities for growth. He, too, had a choice. As soon as my husband became cognizant of his triggers and trauma, he could choose to deal with it all head-on and overcome it, or he could continue to allow them to be his reasons for manipulation. He chose the latter. How he went about dealing with his pain (i.e. lying and cheating) was completely different than the way I was dealing with mine (i.e. food and control). Until I truly understood this, it continued to feel wrong to leave the marriage.

It is not our job to heal someone else's pain. We all go through dark moments in life. That's part of being human. We can be there to support one another; to rally behind those we love to help them see it through to the other side. But it is not our job to heal someone else's pain. We do get to choose, however, whom we let into our lives, who gets to stay, and who needs to go. While it's a tough choice to make, sometimes you have to decide for yourself that you need to cut ties with someone who is holding you back from being and becoming the person you want to be.

When my husband and I reunited, things were going pretty good for a short while but he soon returned to the cycle of lying and cheating. Initially, I was angry. I hated him and felt bad about myself. As usual, I questioned what I had done wrong, and again started asking what I could do to change myself.

And then I took a deep breath and realized that I was not the same person that I was before that last separation. I recognized that while I could not control him or his behavior, and I was not responsible for his choices, I was absolutely responsible for my own, and I could certainly control the decisions I was making for me. I believed at this point that I was no longer that worst version of myself. I knew that I did not want to act or feel that way again. I didn't want to live that pain again. Enough was enough. It was time to move on.

We are all endowed with free will. If you are in a situation that does not feel good, you have the ability to walk away—if that is the right decision for you. If the person you are with is treating you poorly, you can make the choice to go or to stay. If he or she tells you they are going to change and you give them another chance, then they have the free will to either change or not. What you do with the outcome after that is totally within your control. Make the decision for you and no one else. What is best for you? That sounds almost too easy. Love yourself and trust yourself enough to choose. Ultimately, you alone are one hundred percent responsible for your own happiness, health, and wellbeing. As great as it would be to have someone else snap their fingers and make everything right for us, or as awesome as it would be to have a manual of all possible situations and outcomes in life, these things do not exist. What we do have is free will and intuition, and the ability to decide who we want to become, under what conditions, where and with whom we want that to occur.

When you surrender you let go of the distractions going on within and around you. For me, surrendering to the issues with my marriage gave me time and space to clear the chaos and chatter happening in my head. At the time of the final separation. I knew things were different. That I was different. I had to give myself time to learn whatever lessons I needed to learn about myself in order to move on. During that time, I was able to gain some stillness in my life so I could truly open to all the stuff that I needed to deal with. I had done some mindset work up to this point. I had gone to therapy. Some of the pieces were already in place, but it was not until this full and total surrender that I truly realized the full impact of what had happened in the past, why it occurred, and what needed to be done in order for me to turn my life around. Previously, I knew there needed to be a mindset shift, but because of everything that was happening, I didn't really get it.

I had only heard the word "intuition" as a kid. I didn't really understand what it meant until I was a grown up. Nor did I recognize how strong my intuition was until I was well into my thirties. As a kid, I knew things. Rather, I felt things. I was able to perceive the energy around me. If someone was feeling bad, I felt it, too. Intuitively, I knew there was something off. I didn't understand what this energy was. Later in life, I was introduced to a life coach who taught me about empaths. I discovered that I, too, was empathic, and took on the feelings and emotions of others. When I was married, I always knew there was an affair happening, or some lie or deceit. I could feel it. I just chose to ignore it. I didn't trust it.

I was so afraid of being right, and so afraid of making the wrong decision as a result of my being right. I was young, stupid, in love, and scared out of my mind. I was the mom of one, then two, then three, then four tiny babies. I worked off and on, sometimes with a full-time job, but never with anything that had health benefits. And he was employed with a good-paying job and health insurance. I had nowhere to go. Looking back though, I realize that isn't (and wasn't) enough. The thought of leaving left me sad, scared, and feeling alone in the world, and I wasn't confident enough in myself to believe that I could handle it. In truth, I allowed myself to remain blind to the possibilities of what was possible for my life, and in love with the fantasy of the white picket fence, beautiful house, great kids, great job all equating to the formula for a happy life.

What was the actual end-result? I kept riding on a hamster wheel feeling empty inside for the longest time. At first, I believed I needed validation in order to trust my gut. Anytime I sensed something was off, I needed to go on a quest to prove myself right, opening me to the crazy cycle of endless amounts of time checking his cell phone, emails, and asking him to recount every move he took that day. I knew when he was lying, but because I couldn't prove it, I continued to ignore what I was thinking and feeling until those moments came when the proof fell into my lap, and, once again, it felt as though my world was falling apart around me. And the harder I tried to hang on, the more I tried to control him, the further away he pulled.

I concerned myself with the judgements from other people. What would my parents think? What would he tell his parents about me? Would I lose my kids? More fear, which was only a fraction of the problem. I was so concerned with being "more than enough" for everyone around me. I felt a tremendous amount of pressure. I had to juggle all the balls in the air, while changing diapers and making dinner, and making sure the laundry was put away and the house was clean, while working a full-time job and getting the kids to school and activities. It took me years to understand that the chaos came from me feeling that I was not enough. No matter what I did. No matter who I made myself out to be. No matter what shape I sculpted my body. I did not feel or believe that I was enough. Until you can see the value in who you are as a person and a soul and until you choose yourself, you will allow yourself to sustain all sorts of pain and suffering.

I had to come to the realization that I was, and would be, okay on my own. That worrying about his, or anyone else's actions, was hindering my own ability to live a peaceful, happy life. Up to this point, I was in tremendous pain, mentally, physically, emotionally, and even spiritually. I felt sad, depleted, defeated, and disappointed. When feeling that pain became greater than the pain of letting go, when I got so frustrated with myself for feeling so low all the time, and I couldn't take it for another second, I was able to make a different choice.

And there is good news. Change is possible—but only when you decide to kick fear to the curb and take action on whatever it is you really want in life. Change can happen when you start to listen to your intuition; when you pivot.

It does not matter how safe your current situation makes you feel. Safety and comfort are not going to create a purposeful life. You will never truly feel fulfilled if you are living in a state that allows fear to control you. Because the fear is controlling who you are and what you do and what you tolerate for your life. Fear feels heavy and filled with anxiety. Intuition feels light and joyful. These are very different energies and feelings, both in your body and around you. Once you recognize the difference, you can make decisions in a way that support your mission and purpose in life. Fear opens up the possibility for resistance, which leaves you susceptible to the distractions around you, which keeps you standing in the same situation you find yourself in right now.

An example:

I wanted to lose weight. I was afraid of the process to make that happen. What would that look like? What would that feel like? And what would people expect from me when I got to the other side? I made excuses for why I couldn't go to the gym, or why I couldn't eat better, which were distractions. Or, as was sometimes was the case, I would get to the gym, but would sit in the car for thirty-five minutes checking emails or posting on social media and would then complain I had no time to work out because I was so busy with my business (distractions). So, guess what? I stayed overweight. All because I was too scared of the process and what the outcome might look like. While I didn't want to be in pain anymore, I convinced myself that working out was going to hurt too much. I would be so physically uncomfortable that working out would cause too much pain. To avoid that pain, I had to stay in pain because of the weight. A never-ending, vicious cycle.

I wanted a different marriage. I wanted to find a career that I loved. But as was the case with weight loss, I was afraid of the process to make those things happen. Not knowing what the outcome would look like, and continuously reaffirming that it would take a tremendous amount of change on my part is what kept me stuck where I was—feeling hopeless and unfulfilled. What if it was worse than the hell I had already created for myself?

You can never truly run from fear. Even when you start out on your path to change your life, fear is always waiting there behind the next corner. It's always ready to step in and sabotage your next move. The goal is not to get rid of fear completely, rather to learn how to overcome it. To keep things moving even when fear is jumping out to scare you. The only way to do this is to do it. I know—sounds crazy, right? There is no real magic formula. Just action. Once you take that tiny baby step, it's a victory. And that victory will give you momentum to move to the next challenge. And then you keep going from there. It takes time. It takes understanding. And it takes commitment on your part to do the work. You need to be open to recognizing the fear, and then open to pushing it aside and taking action regardless.

CHAPTER 8

Break Time

LET'S TAKE A BREAK FROM our climb, just for a minute, and talk about mindset.

Consider this: What if all of those negative things that you convince yourself to be true about yourself, everything that you believe to be bad, wrong, and broken for your life, are just the things that the world needs more of?

Who are you? What do you want out of life?

Those are huge questions with big answers. But we don't always answer in the most honest fashion.

Sure, there are obvious, easy answers.

- Who am I? I am Liz. I am a mother. I am a wife. I am a business owner. Animal lover.
- What do I want out of life? Love. A house. "That" car. Great hair.

These are one-dimensional responses. And, while there's nothing wrong with these answers, focusing on these things along will present you with a one-dimensional focus to life. Once you surrender, you are letting go of chaos, and detouring away from distraction. It gives you time to distance yourself from the situation and gain some clarity. You will see things in a new perspective, as if with new, fresh eyes. And you start to get a more focused picture of what it is you want in your life. There are deeper answers to these questions, answers that paint a picture of what is going on inside of you, and of what your soul is calling out for. Go deeper. Paint a more complete picture of your life than you ever thought possible.

- Who am I? I am Liz. I am a wife, mother, and business owner. I am an educated woman, who is passionate about helping other people create the life of their dreams. I value friendship, love, peace, family.
- What do I want out of life? I want to live a life feeling confident and strong. I want to help others while living my life to the fullest; I am here to create. To see the world. To laugh. Experience joy.

We could go even deeper, but I think you get the point. I realize that asking yourself these questions can be scary, at least at first. You might not know what to expect, and you might not be too sure if all of the answers are going to be positive. That is okay. You need a starting point, and the awareness of where you are in this moment. With awareness you can make honest decisions about what you want and need, and which direction to take. You gain the freedom to make choices and write a new story for yourself, based on your own rules, values, and desires.

When you ask, "who am I?" take a long, hard, look, and don't be afraid to acknowledge the not-so-nice stuff, too. Your first inclination might be to give the obvious answers. You might even answer in a way that you think you want others want to see you. Or in a way that you believe others already see you. Take those answers and throw them out the window. Dig deep and truly ask yourself, the core you, the child inside who still has some semblance of innocence and who plays and dreams big. It does nobody any good, especially you, to live your life based on how you think someone else wants you to live it. It is your life. Who do you believe you are? Who do you want to be? Be your own guide. And trust that when you ask yourself these questions, you will be guided to the right steps and answers. Trust your intuition and understand that fear will prevent you from having honesty with yourself that these questions demand.

When I first started asking "who am I?" I only gave surface answers, the positive things. Then I got down to business and realized that there was a lot of junk sitting within me.

Who am I?

- I am Liz. Wife. Mother. Business Owner. Educated. Value friendship, peace, family.
- I fear putting myself out there. I care what others think about me and make choices based on those opinions, or what I think those opinions are. I don't feel as though I am enough.

Heavy stuff. It's the stuff that doesn't feel so good; stuff that we might feel resistance to acknowledge or change. Once you start to get open and honest about the heavy stuff, though, you can start to deal with it. Clear it away and see things in a new light. It's an opportunity to take inventory of where you really are in relation to where you want to be and solidify in your mind exactly what you want your life to look like. Paint the picture. Make it so crystal clear that there is no denying it or how it feels. Then make the commitment to yourself that you will bring that picture to life. And believe that you *can!*

When my husband left the final time, I had to make the connection that no matter what I did, I never felt like it was enough. Up until this point I never stopped to consider my own mental state, and what "benefit" I was getting from allowing him to treat me so poorly. Once I got honest with myself, I could start to see my way through it.

Part of this was mindset and the pivot happened when I started to talk differently to myself. Challenge your thoughts. Challenge your reality. Go deep. Then change what you say to yourself. Healthy self-talk is so important. Instead of trash-talking yourself every day, be nice to yourself. Remember that saying "if you don't have anything nice to say then don't say anything at all"—that applies to the things you tell yourself, too. Once you start being kind in what you say to and about yourself, and do it consistently, your actions will soon follow. And you start on the path to changing that mindset.

The change also happened once I took a look back at my life to connect the dots. Understanding from where and whom those deep-seated issues came. Negative thoughts like:

- "I can't change my life."
- "I am not worthy of success."

- "I don't deserve happiness."
- "I will only ever amount to __ in my life."
- "I can't lose weight."

...all kept me from motioning towards what it was I really wanted.

Do you ever catch yourself telling yourself (or someone else) any of the above, or something similar?

Say any or all of those self-limiting beliefs out loud (or in your head) right now. Just the thought of these statements—how do they make you feel? I felt hopeless. Sad. Trapped. Even saying them out loud brings a spirit-crushing kick to the gut. It knocks the wind right out of my sails. These are the types of things we say to ourselves every single day, and the statements that cause us to stay stuck where we are.

Limiting beliefs are all those negative messages that you keep telling yourself throughout your life, and you use them as reasons why you can't do __(insert goals here)__. We acquire limiting beliefs based on our upbringing and the environment in which we are raised and from situations that happen to us when we are kids. We pick them up from cues around us, even the most subtle, and they keep us from taking action and changing our lives. It's time to change all of that.

This is where you pivot.

Make a list of all of those limited beliefs that you have about yourself. To do this, give yourself some time to sit quietly and think about yourself. What comes up? Be totally honest. Think about all of the reasons you tell yourself that you can't do what you want in life. Is it money? Is it time? Do you not feel as though you are good or worthy enough? Write 'em all down. It's going to require brutal honesty. Spoiler alert: this is going to hurt because you are forcing yourself to face all of the lies you tell yourself on a daily basis.

When I first did this activity, I must have had three full pages of limiting beliefs. And I felt sick to my stomach and wanted to run and hide under a rock. But there is no hiding here. This is all about taking the steps needed to live an amazing life.

Once you have written everything out, it's time to change them into something more positive and uplifting for yourself. Flip it over and start again. So instead of telling yourself, "I don't deserve happiness," tell yourself "I am worthy and deserving of love."

Every day you are going to tell yourself these new statements about your life. Do it before you get out of bed or in the car on the commute to work or in the shower. It doesn't matter the time of day, as long as you are consistent about it, and do it even when you don't feel like it or believe it. Over time, you will start to see subtle changes in how you see yourself and the world. You start to create a new story for your life.

It's one thing to *say* you want to live a new life. It's another to actually do the work to make that happen. It requires awareness, self-control, and a level of honesty with yourself that you might have never had before. But first you need to be open to it. You need to allow it. Give yourself permission to create the changes you want to see.

Take action, consistent action, every single day.

Weight loss is the obvious example. Want a better body? We disillusion ourselves to believe that you need to starve yourself and lose one hundred pounds in a week to be successful. We want immediate results. Getting up once every six months to exercise is not going to get you to your goal. Neither is eating nothing but water and crackers for a week. Getting up every single day and walking puts you on the path to a healthier life. Making a conscious effort to eat healthy foods and drink plenty of water is powerful. Consistency is key. This applies to our mindset and what we feed ourselves internally. This applies to us challenging our thoughts, beliefs, and feelings, and connecting them to the situation we are presently in.

There is this notion that in order to be successful you need to take super massive action every day. That simply isn't true. It is unsustainable to expect yourself to take a massive amount of action all the time. This is not a ticket to hit the snooze button and go back to sleep. You still need to do something. But tiny steps will get you to the goal, too. Will it take a little longer? Yes. But if you are not in a place yet where you can take massive action, then know that the little actions add up, too. And it's okay. Be consistent. Just don't stop.

When I started my business, I went through a period where it seemed like it would never happen. The banks kept refusing my loan requests. I couldn't find a production space big enough to do what I wanted to do. I kept feeling like my dream was slipping away. But I kept at it—going back to the drawing board repeatedly, allowing myself to think outside the box of what I had originally envisioned for the business, and realizing that it could happen, but in a different way. It would have never happened without consistency.

There were (and still are) days in my business when I don't feel like it. There are still days when I feel like I don't want to go to the gym. The resistance is going to happen. It's just part par for the course. Still, you must keep moving. Act before you give yourself enough time to think. When you allow yourself to think, you are going to come up with a million reasons to stop yourself.

Be gentle with yourself. It's all a process. If you are waiting for something big to happen—the stars to align, pigs to fly, whatever it is you are waiting for—you'll be waiting for a very long time! You only have one life to live and none of us are guaranteed how many years we get to live it. Don't waste time hoping and dreaming and wishing. Take time to hope, dream, wish, and then DO!

What is one tiny step you can take right now? It does not have to be a big step. But what is one thing? Do it. Right now. That tiny action will help motivate you to the next step. Then the next. And before you know it you have momentum behind you. And you are flying or climbing a mountain. Eventually you will look up and realize that you are no longer the same person you were.

Then, it's time to surrender—again.

What? Why are we going through this again?

As you move forward on your path, you will continue to face new challenges. Each will require you to make a choice: to push past it and keep going, or to stop and let go of the dream or project or idea. There will be reasons, excuses, people—basically, distractions—that will pop up to test your focus. When that happens, surrender again. Recognize the distractions for what they are—fear, excuses, judgement, all creeping back in to try to convince you that your choice to pivot was wrong. That you can't do it or that you shouldn't. Every time social media or the television or the snooze button or the drama with friends or family comes knocking on your door and you lose focus, remember that you choose whether you let that become a distraction. You decide what impact you want it to have on your life. Surrender and pivot again and get back on track towards your goals and dreams.

Remember what you are working toward. And start asking yourself more questions about who you are and what you want. It's possible your desires are changing. It's possible you have hit a block because you are uncovering a new belief that you didn't realize was there before. It's not a one-and-done process. As you continue to evolve, there are going to be days when your mind starts to try to convince yourself that you are going to fail. That you aren't good enough. Maybe you will start to fall back into old patterns. That's when you need to surrender again and be open to change.

CHAPTER 9

And Now, Back to Our Mountain

SURRENDER HAPPENED FOR A FEW weeks after my husband and I reunited. After spending some time apart, we both were able to gain clarity on who we were as individuals, and who we wanted to be as a couple, and we were willing to continue working on things together. Once I surrendered, I was willing to see things differently—not through rose-colored glasses. While I knew that I was not the only issue causing our marriage to fail, I also recognized that a lot of what I was telling myself came from fear and my need for control and my feeling of not being enough. Don't misunderstand me; he was wrong, too. So many people asked me time and time again, "why are you staying?" It took me some time to fully understand it to be able to explain. I recognized he was in pain. I recognized that he was not acting in the way that he said that he wanted to act as a person or as a husband.

After he had come home again, and things had been amazing, I started to fall back into my old patterns. Doubt crept back in. Worry. Fear. And I started to question his every move and motive. What was happening? Hadn't I gotten over all of that? Well, sort of. But I also started taking my career in a new direction. I was also gaining more and more emotional awareness for myself and let me tell you—it's pretty scary and uncomfortable. I needed to surrender again and remind myself that "I am enough" and be willing to see things in a new perspective.

And no matter what things looked like on the outside, this was not an easy decision to make. He was telling me he loved me and acting to the contrary. I was holding onto a hope and a vision for a happy married life, and I loved him, too. And I couldn't ignore the fact that he would continue to come back. There was no magazine quiz that I could take that would give me a definitive answer. It's not easy to decide when you are staring at the person or situation that is presenting itself to you, but also still have a hope and a vision for a life that you dreamt of.

The situation was compounded by those in my life who were telling me to leave him. That I was crazy to stay. That I needed to start over. There were quite a lot of opinions and judgements about what others thought should happen, but nobody ever asked me what I wanted. That made me want to hide from the world even more. I already felt bad about the situation in the marriage, and now had all these people around me trying to give me advice. Friends who disagreed with my decision to stay decided they no longer wanted to associate with me. That did not feel good.

Ultimately, I knew that nobody could make the choice for me. This is the case for pretty much everything that happens in life. Nobody can choose for you. Give yourself and those around you a break. We are all doing the best we can at the time.

There was so much worry and fear. It kept me from fully committing to my marriage, to motherhood, to friendship. I was always expecting something to go wrong. In a sense I had kept one foot out the door, just in case, with pretty much everything. Ironically, I understood that by expecting something to go wrong, I kept looking for things to be wrong. I was choosing the crazy and chaos instead of surrendering and choosing to see what was real and true. I needed to choose to be supportive of myself. I needed to recognize that things could be different—no matter what that different looked like. But I got stuck in the doom and gloom of things and let it stay that way for a long time.

CHAPTER 10

Between Connection and Judgement

AS AN ADULT AND AS A PARENT, I can logically understand that those kids needed a hug or something better to do with their time than to come and tease me. They needed a lesson in awareness and empathy. I can recognize now that their judgement of me reflected their feelings about themselves, their own insecurities, and their own inability to understand emotion. I totally get that we were kids at the time, at a point where these concepts don't tend to make much sense. But even having that logical understanding does not stop me from feeling the pain that their statements caused. That tinge of fear in the pit of my stomach, feeling so bad about myself and feeling as though my looking and being different made me a bad person. I often wonder now if they remember, or if they have any clue how big of an impact those interactions had on my life. And when I think about it, it makes me think about the power that fear of judgement can have over making a connection with oneself and with others, and how judgement stops awareness dead in its tracks, building a huge brick wall between you and the person standing in front of you.

That one experience from my childhood impacted so many experiences and choices throughout my life, making me very much aware of the judgement and walls others were building between me and them, and causing me to build quite a few of my own. The interaction impacted my choices as a parent because I was so afraid and so stuck in a cycle of needing to control every situation around me. While I was doing the best I could, my choices almost cost me my relationship with my daughter. There is this notion that teenagers go from peaceful, nice kids to hell-raisers in the blink of an eye. Going through it with my daughter, I probably would have agreed with this statement. Looking back, I can recognize that her hell-raising days stemmed from the pain and confusion she felt because of the choices I was making in my life. She, too, was very much aware of my husband's behavior, which I didn't know at that time. As she watched events unfold, she didn't know what to believe, or whom to trust. She was scared, and while I was her mom and should have been taking care of her, I was lost in my own issues. Eventually she started acting out, skipped school, began experimenting with drugs, ran away a few times, and wanted to try to be emancipated at the age of sixteen. Between the ages of fourteen and eighteen, the house was chaotic and loud. We spent months in family therapy. Fortunately, we were able to reconnect. But it came only after I was willing and able to hear things from her perspective and understand what she was going through all those years. Before we could be able to find a better connection, we had to tear down the walls of judgement that we had built and start to understand one another in a new way. Or, at least try.

As a mom, it was difficult to hear the things she had to say. But I had to suck it up because I loved my daughter and wanted our relationship to grow stronger. I had to set aside my judgement of her, and of myself, to be open to whatever it was she needed to let go of so that she could heal. Learning to listen became a huge component that I and we had lost.

Recently, I spent the morning with my newborn baby granddaughter, which really made me think about connection. Here is this tiny little newborn, just about a month old. And all she wants is food, warmth, a clean diaper, and snuggles. If she stirs or even if she is crying her head off, she easily calms down once she knows there is another person there with her. She grabs onto your finger with her tiny little hand for dear life. She wants to know she is safe. She is looking for connection.

Connection is a necessary part of life—no matter how old you are. We need one another. Let's imagine for a second that you just won the lottery, you have the best job in the entire world, and have all of the material possessions you have ever wanted. Would all those gifts be as fun to have if you weren't able to share them with others? Likely not. None of that seems to matter if we're alone. Connection helps us to feel happy and fulfilled. Connection is also important in helping us talk through difficult decisions or work on a challenging project. It creates new opportunities for collaboration.

Thinking back to my childhood, I remember those moments when we were all gathered around the table, and I always wondered why that meant so much to me. Even as a parent, having dinner every night as a family was something that brought me such joy—the opportunity to connect with people who love.

As humans we all need connection and love, but the reality is that we live in a world full of judgement. We are quick to tear one another down, and not always as quick to raise one another up. It can be scary and risky to do so. What if the person next to us rises, and then climbs beyond us? Will they surpass us on the path and leave us behind? Maybe. This fear causes us to create judgements that allow us to believe that others are (insert random negative here) and are therefore not worthy of success and happiness. I've heard it so many times from others. And, yes, I've done it, too. It goes a little something like this:

- "I can't believe he/she got that promotion/raise/accolade!"
- "He or she is so __!" (insert random list of negative words, actions that we attribute to the person).
- "I deserve it more because..."

And all the while, with the above going on, either in our heads, or standing with a group of co-workers at the water cooler, we are outwardly clapping and giving a tight smile, as we grin and bear what's happening right in front of us.

In the age of social media, though, "connection" is such a loaded word, and we correlate connection with the number of likes on our posts. In some ways, it's a lot easier to share details with social media acting as a veil of protection. It doesn't matter who is reading and if they are judging us. You don't see or feel that judgement (unless they comment on your feed). If they don't like or comment, they don't like or comment. You can't see their reactions. But is it authentic? Somewhat and sometimes, but not always. Let's not forget that there is a ton of value in creating real, vulnerable relationships with those who occupy the same physical space at the same time.

We have real relationships happening in front of our faces (away from the computer screen). But we move further away from those live interactions. We text or send an email instead of making a phone call. We are more willing to interact in a chatroom setting than a real world setting. I think about all the times I told my kids to call their friends to make plans to hang out, and my request being met with looks of confusion and dread. Nobody calls anymore. This has caused a major shift in society and not completely for the better. I cannot ignore the fact that tech has greatly impacted previous social norms. I observe those who are more engaged in their smartphone than they are interested in live conversation, board games, good old-fashioned play. Disconnecting from technology, even for a few minutes, seems to be a challenge. Of course, I see a need and value in the progress of technology but at what cost? Where's the balance?

It's frustrating to think that there are companies out there that have adopted and encourage this type of interaction. I used to work for a company that highly discouraged any one-to-one interaction among co-workers and required you to submit a work ticket to ask any questions of your supervisors via the computer. Even if your supervisor sat in the cubicle next to you. While this is a rare and extreme (I hope) example, it happens in the world today. As more companies go virtual, using technology to interact becomes a necessity. But I would argue that there are ways to create comradery and cohesion and connection even while using the tools of tech. I thought about this the other day as I was waiting for a cup of coffee from a local convenience store. I was watching the people behind the counter, working fast and furious to feed the hungry crowd in front of them, but none of the employees looked at any of the customers. They had to keep their head down, work fast, and only glance up just enough to peek at the computer monitor on the wall showing the next order. There was no connection with the customer. No engagement. Not even a "thank you." We go into this store all the time and use a computer to enter our order. This company uses this system in all of their locations. And the experience is always the same. Go in. Push a few buttons to order. Pay. Get your stuff and get out. As a society, we have come to accept and tolerate this type of experience.

As a businesswoman, I understand that it costs time and money and resources to have employees engage with customers. You have to train them on the processes. You have to train them to answer the questions or handle situations in a way that aligns with the corporate mission and vision. And the longer it takes to train them to do that, the longer it takes for them to be able to be on the floor, head down, making sandwiches and handing out iced coffee so that the company can put cash in the register. Recognize that we have accepted this. Even some of the biggest online companies make it difficult to connect with a live person. Do you shop online? Have you ever had an issue with your online purchase? Have you ever tried to find a customer service phone number on that company's website? Often it's buried somewhere deep in the site. Sometimes it's not there at all. Sometimes your only option is sending an email. Sometimes your only option is a chat bot. We get frustrated with it and complain about it, but we have accepted it enough that we choose to spend our money in these types of places instead of with companies who really want to interact, engage, and connect with the people who support them.

As a consumer, this type of system brings out our impatience. We want it yesterday. There's no need to wait when we can go online and .com it and have it on our doorstep within a matter of hours. This is where I implore you to pivot. Recognize that there could be a different way. Recognize that we need connection. To ourselves. With other people. Even in business. Get up and personal with life.

I am not advocating the avoidance of social media, or that we dismantle technology as we currently know it, but maybe a little less screen time, and a little more reaching out to those around you. Or perhaps, finding new ways to use this amazing technology to create connection, awareness, and understanding in the world. So many of us equate our self-worth with the number of social media friends we have, or the number of likes our social media posts gain. That is a big lie that we allow ourselves to indulge in. We all want to be like. To feel loved. To feel valued and valuable. While we want others to think it, it's more important that we believe it for ourselves. You have nothing to prove to the world. You are not the number of likes or comments. You are more than that. Bigger than that. Regardless of whether or not one person or ten thousand people like, love, or laugh at your content, you are valuable and valued in this world. Please do not ever forget that. And please don't allow yourself to get stuck believing that someone else gets to decide your worth.

Look down your list of friends on Facebook. Are you truly friends with every single one? Do they "get" you? Do they align with your vibe? Maybe. Maybe not. It's difficult to tell, really, because when you are online, you can be whomever it is you want to be. Yet, for some reason, many of us feel inclined to share about our personal lives on social media. But getting social online puts a veil of security over our faces. We can feel free to share more of ourselves because we don't see the reactions of those on the other end of the conversation. When was the last time you shared something deep and meaningful on your Instagram or Facebook feed? Did you stop for a second before hitting "post" to consider how the message would be received? If it would offend anyone? Did you think about the fact that anyone reading the post would likely make a judgement or decision based on that post? How much do you care about any of that?

Let's give one another a break, both online and in person. If we took a minute to put ourselves in someone else's shoes and stopped judging them because of how they think, the world might be a happier place. Without the judgement we allow ourselves and each other the freedom to be expressive and to have empathy for ourselves and for others. And it allows for more understanding of others. We can all coexist peacefully in this world, and not tear ourselves, or one another apart.

Do you know what the person sitting next to you is currently dealing with or what they have lived through? Maybe your coworker that you have been judging is in a troubled marriage and she could really use a friend to help her through it. Maybe the kids you are judging as "stupid" are having some trouble in school and could use some help. Maybe that woman sitting in the coffee shop that you are judging is a new mother and only got an hour of sleep last night because she was taking care of the baby. Maybe that guy that you are judging just lost his job and is trying his best to get food on the table to feed his family.

In truth, we are so quick to judge ourselves, and often, we are much harder on ourselves than we would ever be to another human being. And when you are your own harshest critic, of course it can be difficult to speak your truth out loud. That self-judgement is preventing you from being your authentic self—from breaking free to live the life you want to live, as the person you want to be.

What do we do about self-judgement? How do we break out of that cycle? Having an awareness is a good first step. Recognize those moments when you get stuck in that self-judgmental mindset. What are you telling yourself? That you are wrong? Bad? Made a mistake? Aren't good enough? We have no problem identifying our own areas of perceived lack or limitation. This is so destructive to our lives and to all that we dream of accomplishing. Let's try a little experiment. Think about something that you have done that has gone right in your life. Give yourself a pat on the back. How does that feel? It might feel weird at first but make this a habit and over time it will feel better and better and you will be able to own that sense of contentment and fulfillment.

I don't know about you, but I grew up being taught that you don't brag or boast about yourself. You keep that to yourself. Got an "A" on the test? Don't tell anyone. Won an award? Nobody else needs to know. Been working hard on a project that you completed and are really proud of? Great job, but again, let's not talk about it. However, if I ever did something wrong, well, I knew it, and so did everyone else around me. I didn't want to create anything new or special for my life. Why would I? I was taught not to celebrate it, and there was only people around to tell me all the ways I did it wrong.

Connection is as much about interacting with ourselves, with nature, with our immediate surroundings, as it is about having a deep and meaningful conversation with the person sitting next to us. Reach out to nature and take a walk and listen to the birds. Spend time journaling and interact with your own thoughts and feelings so you can understand your own views of the world. Read a book to understand the views and opinions of other people or use your imagination to understand someone else's story. Meditate and breathe for even as little as five minutes a day. Disconnect to connect. You would be amazed at how your world will expand when you open yourself up to the possibilities. You begin to understand what and who you want to be in life.

Anytime we choose to learn and grow we need to be prepared for things to change—one way or another. It takes courage to change your part of a relationship system, but it is so worth it!

This includes the relationship with those naysayers around you, as well as with those who are there to support you. More importantly, it refers to the relationship you have with yourself. It's already been said, but it's worth repeating: We can't control other people. We can only control ourselves. So, it's up to us to individually put a stop to the chronic judgement that exists in the world. Acknowledge it. Be aware of it. Then choose again.

Even with all the junk that was going on when I was a kid, and as easy as it is to blame the people around me, it was nobody else's fault. My parents were doing the best that they could at the time. Same with the kids around me. I have come to a point now where I don't blame any of them, truly. The path was my choice to take. Though the lessons might have been learned the hard way, they were mine to learn. Now it's time to move on and choose again.

It's time to celebrate you! Celebrate life! Celebrate the wins, no matter how big or small. What is going well right now with you and with your life? Even if it's something small or that we take for granted—you've managed to pay rent this month, you've maintained your health and wellness, you have a kind disposition. Are you able to answer that question? Here is where the pivot happens. Start right now by telling yourself even one amazing and fantastic thing about yourself. You have to start somewhere. Pivot and make the choice to stop judging yourself in such a cruel and harsh manner and choose to see the good in yourself. After you get used to the feeling of celebrating that one good thing, start thinking about all of the other things that make you fantastic. Because you are. And you need to feel it, believe it, and live it-regardless of how many people look at, comment on, or like anything you write on social media.

And guess what?

When you make that shift for yourself, and you start to celebrate the goodness in you, you start to give those around you a break, too. There's that saying, "be the change you want to see in the world." Well, here's your shot. It starts with you. Choose to ignore that voice inside of you that says it's wrong to celebrate the good stuff. Be nice to yourself and let yourself celebrate your victories. Smile. Cheer. Do the happy dance. Hug it out. Even say to yourself "this ___ went right today and I nailed it." You will be amazed at how a small shift can make big changes for you, in how you see yourself, and in how you see the world around you.

As a side note, when you start to see changes in your life, acknowledge that change is possible for those around you, too. Give the other people in your life the breathing room they need, and believe that they can do it, too. It likely isn't going to look the same as your change. It likely won't go at the same pace as yours. It might go faster or slower. Your friends and family are on their own path, making their own choices, and doing the best that they can do in the present moment. No two pivots are identical, and that's okay. Be there to support and encourage them, remembering what it feels like to so desperately want to create change, and not realize how to gain traction for the cause.

If you look for all of the good stuff in your life, you end up attracting more of that goodness. What you focus on will grow. So, focus on the good and create more of that for your life. When you do that, out of love for yourself, things seem to fall into place around you. That holds true for the people around you as well. We can choose to climb the mountain alone or with people around us. It's a lot more fun and a lot easier to climb with ten of your best and closest friends.

That said, when you are truly connected and aligned with your true self, when you know intuitively who you are, the noisy chatter of life tends to fall away making it easier to connect with those around you. When the chaos and crazy in your mind quiets down, you free up the energy and resources to tune in and listen and allow yourself to be fully present in the moment. It forges a connection that is undeniable. There's power in that.

Camp 3: Career

AS A KID I WANTED TO START my own bakery. As an adult, as I started the planning process for my bakery, I planned one that aligned as best as I could with the vision that I had when I was a child. A beautiful storefront. Lovely equipment. A case full of beautiful pastries. And customers lined up out the door for days.

That is not how it began. It did not start out exactly the way I intended, or in the way that I wanted it to be. In the earliest days of my bakery business, I found a business incubator where I could rent production space. Just enough for a few production tables, ingredient racks, an oven, and me. There was no storefront. I had to find another way to get my product out to the public. I spent eighteen months working between six and eight farmer's markets a week, trying to sell some cookies and build a wholesale client base. It was not the 1500-square-foot retail store I envisioned. And while we developed a solid customer base, we certainly did not have lines of customers. My first farmer's market was a huge flop. I was learning how to use new equipment and scale up the recipes. My packaging looked horrendous. My first showing was not at all strong. I felt like a failure. I looked at my husband and felt like I was letting him and the kids down. I expected it to happen all at once. That I would open up at that first farmer's market to a long line of customers just waiting for some cookies. MY cookies. And my company would be a huge, amazing, overnight success. At that time, I believed that if that did not happen, I was a failure. That I was wrong to start a business. That I would never make it happen. My failure on day one made me question my ability to even bake a cookie, which is something I had done for years by this point. The self-doubt crept in—hard.

Eventually, I had to shake off the doubt, ignore the negative chatter that was happening in my brain, and work. I could either sit there and let the self-doubt bring me down, turn off the ovens, and never bake again, or I could push through the discomfort, adapt to the fact that this was a challenge, and allow myself the time and space to grow. I chose to keep going. I chose to pivot.

After about eighteen months, I was working hard, and I loving every second of it. After I started hosting in-home birthday parties, I knew I wanted to branch out with my own retail space that I could call home, offering fresh-baked treats, as well as birthday parties and cooking classes. At the time that I had moved into my own store, I had gotten my weight down to around 320 pounds, I still had a long way to go (both internally

THIS IS WHERE YOU PIVOT

and externally). I somehow could not get a handle on things enough to get down to the weight I really wanted to be at. I was in a rocky marriage, with four teenagers running around, and owning a business. I was doing a lot of things, and there were always people around me, but still I felt extremely lonely. The life of an entrepreneur—while many think it's fun and glamorous, it comes at a cost. When I opened, I believed that *I* was the business. I lived it, breathed it, and was never quite able to turn it off (I later came to realize that this was not true, but more on that later). As far as my weight went, there were some (minimal) efforts made. I went to the gym. I made dinner from scratch. Did I work out as hard as I should have? No. Were those meals always well-balanced and lean? No. And at the end of the night, when I was left to my thoughts, I needed a cookie. Or a piece of cake. Something sweet. When the girls finished their winter concert, we needed to celebrate with a cookie or a cake. When the kids brought home report cards with good grades, we went out for ice cream. And after a big fight with the hubs, all I wanted was a brownie. I could keep going, but I think you get the point.

There I was, living a dream I had had for so long. After running the storefront for almost a year, I was still finding myself feeling stuck. Again, recognizing a feeling of discontent, I was still dealing with the same demons I had prior to my launch. And I came to a soul-shocking revelation: I realized that I was living a life that I had created because of someone else's expectations and opinions of me. I was a baker because I wanted people to like me. I was a baker because at some point in my life someone told me I made great cookies. I was a baker to give myself an excuse to stay overweight. I was running this particular business to distract me from the other stuff that I was trying so desperately to change.

That all sounds so counterintuitive. Why would anyone do that? Logically, it doesn't make sense. The quest for a fulfilling life of purpose is one of the heart and not of the head. Deep down, I felt that I could magically get people to like me and pay attention to me if I fed them and kept them happy with food, while giving myself a reason to eat and taste and enjoy with them, which also kept me overweight and hiding from the world. And if I was running this business, I wouldn't have to deal with what was going on at home.

Eventually, I had to stop and ask myself why I was doing it. I had to consider where I had managed to take the business, compared to my initial dreams and expectations, I had to stop and also look at my behavior and connect it to the resistance I felt to doing the things that I would have needed to do in order to achieve that success. I was successful in owning the business. But I could have had even bigger success had I chosen to take more action. Looking back to the time I was in culinary school; I can see that I was already putting limitations on my business and talking about the things I wasn't willing to do. I told classmates that I didn't ever want to be a wedding cake designer and was more than happy just creating the perfect cookie or brownie for people to enjoy. I limited my business years before it had even begun. I limited my own skills and abilities before I had the chance to show myself what I could do. Once I examined the resistance, I realized I was not doing what truly made *me* happy. I enjoyed it, but it was also draining. Getting up at 3 a.m. didn't make me happy. Working eighteen hours a day didn't make me happy. Neither did purchasing supplies, taking inventory, marketing, or worrying about negative reviews popping up on social media. I could have hired someone to help with those tasks, but again, I was in a space of limitation and couldn't see the possibilities of what could be. It didn't light me up enough to take it beyond sustainable. Once I realized this, I started examining things from a new perspective. I got to a place within myself where I could ask myself "what else is possible?" I knew that I *could* do it (i.e. start and run a successful business). I just spent months proving it to myself. So what path could I choose instead, that would create that fulfilment I was seeking?

There have been so many times in my business where that self-doubt crept in. I still must remind myself that those moments are clues for my path. There were many points, especially in the early days, that I distinctly remember telling my husband "I never want to feel like this again." In those moments it was time to look at what was working and what wasn't and find ways to take new actions. Do something different. Just keep moving.

Maybe there is something you need to tweak. Allow yourself those moments of reflection so you can pivot and course correct. Consistent action is key. And I've said it before, and I will say it again—do not ever quit. Things don't always happen in a linear fashion or in the way we expect or plan them to. You make requests of the universe and you ask for what you want. But be open to allowing it in whatever way it comes to you.

If you want to pursue the life of your dreams, you need to be relentless about it—so focused on it that there is no other alternative. BUT be open to the multiple ways that it can happen. The *how* of it does not need to be so black and white. Success does not need to come in a linear, straight-line fashion (and likely won't). There are going to be highs and lows. Expect the peaks and valleys. It's part of the process. Know your desired outcome and be open and receptive to all of the ways that that outcome can occur. Having open-minded thinking gives you so many more options. Don't limit yourself. When you start limiting yourself and your process, you limit your success. And you deserve massive success in whatever shape or form that looks like for you.

What happens once you have made the choice to pivot?

That, my friends, is where the magic begins.

One day during a workout in the gym, I came to understand the fact that we all like to make things so difficult for ourselves. I was on the stepper machine, and, though I tried hard not to, I let myself look at the time that had passed. Immediately, I got winded and thought "oh my gosh, this is getting so hard, I need to stop." This had happened to me before, and maybe you have had this happen to you, too. You psyche yourself out into thinking, "this is just too difficult; I need to stop; I can't do this."

And then, you pivot!

Here's how this scenario played out for me that day. Are you ready?

I didn't stop; I simply slowed myself down.

Once you choose beyond your current situation, you allow yourself to open to so many more possibilities for your life. It is simple, but it's not easy. You have to take action. And action requires you to continue to overcome those demons in your mind. That can be overwhelming. You might tell yourself, "this is too hard; I need to stop; I can't do this." When that happens, slow down. Give yourself time to catch your breath, but never stop moving forward.

CHAPTER 12

Camp 4: Gratitude

WE GET UP IN THE MORNING and start judging ourselves the second we look in the mirror. I bet you have said any one of these statements to yourself before:

"I am so fat." "I have so many wrinkles." "These jeans look terrible on me." Unnecessary judgement.

How many of us stop ourselves from having experiences in life, from experiencing joy and pleasure, because of that judgement? Have you ever refused to go swimming because you felt uncomfortable putting on a swimsuit in front of another person? If you are judging yourself you are holding yourself back, limiting your potential, and limiting the possibilities for your life.

As a child and even well into my grown-up years, I would sit at the Thanksgiving table waiting for my turkey and think about what I was thankful for. I wish I could say that I understood the meaning behind what I was saying when I was a kid. But back then, expressing gratitude on Thanksgiving was more of an obligation to get to eat dinner than a feeling that was expressed. In reality, I started to understand gratitude and its purpose and power about two years ago. I found a group of individuals who were practicing gratitude on a daily basis. Taking a moment to acknowledge something in their life, even in those darkest moments, helped them find peace. For some, it was their spouse. Others, their pets. For some, they were grateful to be recovering from a major life crisis or illness. Some were grateful simply for the gift of living another day. I learned about a gratitude challenge where participants are invited to express gratitude for one thing in their live every single day for thirty days. Some took the challenge out to forty-five or sixty days. Before this group I didn't understand how powerful expressing gratitude could be. I can't count the number of days that went by in my life that I had my head down in the dumps, crying, sad, depressed, and feeling like there was a weight sitting on my shoulders that I could not carry anymore. I suffered with depression for years. Attempted suicide twice. When other group members shared some of their daily gratitude with me, I had two eye-opening revelations. One: there is always something to be grateful for. Second: my life is not all that bad.

Gratitude is the opposite of judgement.

Recognizing that things were not so bad does not mean that we don't or shouldn't feel the pain in our lives. While I say that life is not all bad, life can still be a challenge. Pain and suffering is real. But we get to choose to let that pain and suffering turn become permanent doom and gloom, or we can choose to see it in another way. We can seek to understand the lesson we need to learn from the situation and use it to help us grow.

It's counterintuitive, I know. It's easy to be grateful for the good stuff that happens to us. It's a bit more challenging to be grateful for the bad. But by choosing to find that silver lining, it frees us. There is freedom in that pivot. Freedom in that moment when you make the choice. You are saying "I will no longer let this negative situation control my life." It goes hand in hand with forgiveness. You forgive to free yourself. To break the chains of your own suffering, so that you can continue to learn and grow and see progress in your own life. Even in the times when things seem the hardest, look for something to be grateful for. It can be as simple as having gratitude for the sun coming up that day, but it gives you something to smile about. And that subtle shift changes the energy within and around you. Suddenly, things don't seem to be so bad. It lightens that burden.

When I started to understand gratitude, I began with one thing every day to be grateful for. Then I would list ten things every single day. I started my day with gratitude and found it to make a huge difference in my mindset. Coming home after a long and stressful day, I could come back to my gratitude list and count my blessings, which helped ease some of the stress and tension I was feeling.

Later, I came to see gratitude in an even more powerful way. Eventually, I was able to express gratitude for all the garbage that my husband put me through. All of the manipulation. All of the lies. All of the excuses and broken promises. I was grateful for all of it. I realize that that might not make sense logically, but it made all of the difference in the world. My journey with my husband made me who I am today. That journey gave me the push I needed to turn my life around. To make the decision to not stay stuck. To choose another path. While I started on the mindfulness path believing I was changing myself to better my marriage and make my husband love me and stay committed, in truth, in the end, I was able to improve myself so that I found love and appreciation for myself and wanted to stay committed to me and my own happiness. How could I not be grateful for that? That journey set me on a path to taking new risks, making changes, and deciding I no longer was willing to live a small life, hiding in the shadows. It allowed me to recognize that I was more powerful and capable than I ever believed in the past.

Gratitude is incredibly powerful. In a moment of sadness or challenge, when everything else seems to be falling apart, gratitude can make or break the situation. It gets us out of our heads and into our hearts. When I think about all I am grateful for I feel rich, lucky, and blessed. It's more than words. It's an emotion that transforms mindset almost instantaneously.

This is where you pivot.

What do you have to be grateful for in your life right now? Write it down. Don't just think about it. Feel it, too. And connect with the "why" behind the gratitude. For me, I think about my kids. I am so grateful to be their mom and so grateful for the opportunity to watch them grow and learn. And I am grateful for the lessons that they teach me. Thinking about them puts a smile on my face. I stand a little taller and feel a sense of pride for my family.

I am grateful for my body. Ladies and gentlemen—the struggle is real, even now after all this time. My body is not perfect. But when that mountain called "body image" peeks above the horizon, I remind myself that I gave birth to four kids and that I work hard. This body hiked a mountain called "childbirth" and survived to tell the tale! And I am grateful for its beauty, its imperfections, and all its strength.

Holding that gratitude in my heart each day makes me want to make better choices for myself. That includes (but is not limited to) matters of food, exercise, sleep, and de-stressing. That said, that gratitude also helps me to be a little kinder to myself on the days when my best-laid plans go out the window. It's about progress, not perfection and my pivot happens each time I find myself starting to beat myself up for not pushing harder. I can make a different choice. I choose to be grateful, and that knocks the negative self-talk right off of the mountain, clearing the path for me to continue on my journey with a more peaceful mindset.

I am grateful for my husband. I am grateful for the life we share together, and for the lessons that we have taught one another about life, love, and forgiveness. In truth, his behavior was rotten. You know this now. I know it. And, yes, even he knows it. And I am grateful for it. Without having gone through any of that, I can't say that I would have the understanding and awareness that I have today. Some of the experiences I have had, the lessons I have learned, and some of the people in my life have shown up as a direct result of choices I made because of what was happening in our relationship.

Gratitude doesn't always have to revolve around some deep, complicated lesson of life, and it doesn't have to involve another person. I am grateful for the sun. I love sitting outside on a sunny day and am so grateful to feel the warmth of the sun on my face. I love chai tea and am grateful for how a cup of it makes me feel a sense of comfort and calm. It really can be that simple.

These are just a couple of examples. What are you grateful for? The good, the bad, and the ugly. Why? What impact has that person or situation had on your life?

Here's the thing...gratitude is not exclusively related to positive experiences. The minute you can find gratitude for the not-so-good stuff, you open the possibility for a shift to occur.

Live with gratitude and you will experience joy and peace. When you are grateful for everything, you live a life of complete and total magnificence. How can there be any other alternative when you are grateful for it all? Make your life easy. Find the points where you need and want to pivot, and then make the choice to do so and be grateful for the ability to make the choice. You do not have to stay stuck where you are. You are one-hundred percent capable of change, of movement, of progress. You simply need to make the decision to do so. And you are so worth it. Believe that you are worth the change. The world needs you and we are grateful for you!

CHAPTER 13

Summit: This is Where You Pivot

BY NOW, YOU MIGHT FIND YOURSELF thinking "wait, Liz. I thought we were climbing a mountain."

You are right, my friends, our journey together started with me screaming and crying my way up that mountain. The journey of the climb gave me a remarkable shift in perspective. Each step up, much like the steps we take through life, is a test of endurance. Every step along the journey is like the next obstacle that we are all bound to face in our lives. The question becomes: will you rise up to meet the challenge? And if so, how?

One foot in front of the other. One deep breath at a time; pushing and pulling my way to the top. I decided I was going to get there. One way or another. I wanted to see this waterfall. I was going to make it. There was no other choice. I decided to kick my fear in the face and climb this mountain. I was not under any circumstance going to let fear kill me that day. I had to remind myself exactly what I was climbing back for. I had to believe in myself with every ounce of my being because there was no other alternative than to get back to safety. This is where you pivot!

When we got to the top and I was able to rest, I collapsed onto a rock. I was exhausted. Maybe a little bit in shock, completely overwhelmed with emotion, unable to speak, a little angry with my husband for taking me on this journey, a little grateful with my husband for taking me on this journey, and in complete awe of the beauty of what was right in front of me. I was sitting next to a waterfall and I had just climbed a mountain. I was truly speechless.

Why had I been so afraid? Even though we were at the top, we still had to get back down the mountain. I had no idea what the downward side was going to look like. Surely, I couldn't be the only one who realized the danger.

On the way down, I realized just how difficult I made the experience for myself. My fear caused such a resistance to the experience. It took longer for me to get where I needed to go and longer to make a decision. I kept choosing the longer path, creating more fear, which kept me stuck in fear for more time than necessary. In trying to stay off of the edge of the cliff, I pretty much glued myself as far away from that side of the path as possible, which meant scraping myself up against the rocks and roots of the trees, and usually picking rocks that were harder to get footing on. In my mind, though, as long as I stayed away from the edge of the cliff, and didn't look in that direction, I was going to be okay. I ended up climbing the mountain, literally, crawling. My husband told me it was called "tripoding." I couldn't bring myself to stand up and get the job done.

There was a moment sitting by the water that I was so angry at my husband that I wanted to yell and scream at him; angry that he would bring me here. I wanted to blame him for causing my discomfort. I was doing just fine causing that discomfort for myself. I was giving my power to that mountain, just as I had given my power away to all of those who mocked, judged, and ridiculed me up to this point.

In that moment came the pivot. It's a mountain each and every one of us climbs every day of our lives. Which direction do we choose? That moment was a pivot.

Choosing love. Choosing peace. Choosing calm. Choosing to walk myself down from the mountain with confidence. Choosing beyond fear. Choosing beyond judgement. For once, I was going to lean in and let myself have that victory.

Once I made the choice, I finally started taking the path of least resistance. Calmly and collectively looking for the next best right step. Which rock? Which direction? Strategically, confidently, calmly getting myself out. I also started to enjoy the process a lot more. Laughing. Joking. Taking deeper, cleaner breaths. Settling into the moment and being truly present instead of thinking that the next step I took was going to plummet me to my impending and untimely death.

Pivot... Away from fear. Away from the crazy-town. Away from judgement. Away from blame.

What would you do if you could do anything? What would you do that serves you in the most profound way, to bring you the most joy and peace? Why are you not doing it? In a sense, you, too, like me, are crawling instead of climbing up your mountain. Give yourself time and space to acknowledge whatever that thing is that stirs your soul and makes you come alive. That "thing" will bring you such joy that it makes resistance towards the other not-so-easy parts of life fall away. It does not need to be your paid career. You can do it for the love of sharing that passion with the world. You can even do it solely for the fact that you love to do it. Period. No other persons of interest are required for you to do something that makes you happy. Just know that when you are doing "that thing" that it will spark a light in you so bright, that others will be attracted to come along with you on your journey. Are there ways that you can bring that passion to life right now? Focus on living a meaningful life.

Your life starts the second you acknowledge your flaws and imperfections and choose to love yourself anyway. Honor your thoughts, feelings, intuition. Embrace your true self and make decisions based on what is going to bring you the most joy, peace, and happiness. Life begins when you decide that you are in the driver's seat and you are going to take care of yourself.

So how did I get myself out?

First, there had to be awareness. I had to recognize that what was happening was one hundred percent fear. Then I had to take a deep breath and choose how I was going to handle the situation and find a way to redirect. I was the only one who could control the situation. Being stuck in fear kept me in the most danger. I remember singing a lot. It helped me to distract my mind from thinking "holy cow, I am about to die." I kept thanking the trees for their guidance and support. Feeling immense gratitude that they were strong enough to help me pull myself up and through the trek was helpful. I prayed.

Second, acknowledge that it's not always pleasant. It's a challenge. It's a climb. There's a broad spectrum of emotions throughout the journey. Feel the feelings. Honor them. Good. Bad. Sad. Angry. Feel it. Talk about it. Then you can let it go and keep moving.

Eventually, you land exactly where you were intending to go. At that moment, you look back from the other side of the mountain and tell yourself "that wasn't so bad after all." Time to celebrate the success.

Pivot! The view is so much better once you do it! Don't waste time and energy on self-doubt or fear. Just pivot. Choose love. Choose your own freedom.

Choose to see the beauty in the moment rather than stay stuck on the irrational. This is where you pivot. With every pivot comes transformation. Make a new, different choice for yourself. One by one. Each new choice creates a slightly modified version of the life you are living. Eventually, you will no longer be the same person you see in the mirror today.

Pretending to be something you are not is *not* living your truth. That is living someone else's version of you. Stand in your own light and be confident in who you are. If it does not feel right for you, acknowledge that. Be grateful for that awareness. Then, let it go. Rewrite the old stories that you allow to limit your experience in this lifetime. What will your new story say?

Become crystal clear on the outcome you desire. Then, focus on your why. Why do you want that? What would it mean for you? Your family? What action steps do you need to take to achieve it? Plan the next path of your life story.

What did you have to go through to get where you are today? What lessons; what kind of pain? Express gratitude for those experiences and start to see them as the lessons you needed to create the change. Set yourself free from the pain those times caused you. Forgive. Let go. Recognize that those experiences were lessons for you to learn, so that you could grow and blossom into the incredible person you are right now. Know that more experiences are coming down the path to help you continue to bloom. You might struggle through some of them, or even all of them. It's okay if that happens. The struggle helps us recognize our strength.

Acknowledge your unique gifts. Acknowledge that there is nobody else on this planet that is exactly like you. No one. Think about that for a second. There is only one you. Take care of yourself because when you take care of you, you make the world a more beautiful place. It starts with you. We can't control what happens in the world but we can choose to create peace and harmony in our own lives, and that peace echoes into the far reaches of the universe. And when you are confident, standing at the top of your own mountain, overcoming fear, and living your truth, there is absolutely nothing that can stop you. When you are living from that space, things have a way of falling into place, exactly as they should.

The day my son graduated from high school I had an existential crisis. There I was, forty years old watching my baby boy walk across the stage to get his diploma, and the last eighteen years flashed before my eyes. His first words. Hearing him sing to his little sister. Every argument. Every funny moment. Every homerun or breathtaking play at third base, right up until his varsity baseball team lost the state championship in the first round of the tournament. I saw him get on the bus for his first day of kindergarten right up to the day he was accepted to high school, and the day he was signed to play baseball in college. Eighteen years. Truly a blink of an eye. My heart was overflowing with emotion. I was sad that he was "leaving the nest" so to speak, and excited to see how he would take his place in the world.

Then, reality smacked me right in the face.

I was suddenly very much more aware of time (I never really listened as a kid), and it truly does fly. For a moment, and for the first time, I felt "old," with the staggering realization that none of us are guaranteed a set number of days in this lifetime. I had heard this before, and I am pretty sure I have said it in this book already, so I know you have heard it, too. But, truly, it hadn't struck me with quite as much clarity as it did that day. None of us ever know when we will take our final breath.

I didn't feel very well that night. I lay awake with an eerie anxiety that left me hearing a rambling beat of "tic toc" in my mind. I got the message—the clock keeps moving. Time is ticking away.

Did I love him (my son) enough? Did I teach him the right lessons? Will he remember to set his alarm to wake himself up for class or to do his laundry while he was away at college? The entire day made me think long and hard. Was I using my time wisely?

This makes it more important to me that everyone on the planet recognizes that they have the power to pivot. How are you using your time in your life? Are you creating those magical, wonderful memories for yourself and your family? Are you living a life that *you* created for yourself, or one that was created for you?

CHAPTER 14

Final Thoughts

THANK YOU FOR COMING ALONG on this journey with me. Before we part, I must ask you: what mountain are you climbing? For each of us the mountain looks different. Maybe you are in a career transition. Maybe you are a new parent. Or just graduated from college. Maybe you are battling depression or diabetes or addiction. No matter the mountain, this is where you pivot towards new choices, new pathways, and new opportunities. This is where you find peace. This is where you find joy. Know that you have everything within you to find your way, and in those times when you are struggling to believe in yourself, there are people out there, ready and willing to help push you up your mountain when you need it. Though sometimes the light on the path seems dim and you feel that you are making the trek by yourself, please know that you are never alone.

Be patient with yourself and with others. Be kind and giving, but don't give all of yourself away so that you have nothing left to give yourself.

Blessings and happiness and success to you. We are on this mountain together. Let's do this.

Post Script

And in case anyone was wondering, about a month after this ridiculous hike, the trail was closed. Too many people were injured on the trail and the state decided it was time to close it to keep people out of harm's way. While I am massively grateful that I went on the trip and took part in that hike, I can't help but think about that warning sign at the start of the trail. There are times when one should consider the trail's closing to be a sign that it's okay to not make the climb. Listen to your intuition if something seems off. I am not advocating avoiding the work. Going after your dreams can be scary, and takes time, effort, and the willingness to overcome the resistance inside of you. But please know that, sometimes, it's okay to find a way around the mountain, rather than try to climb over it.

Fear and intuition feel and sound very different. But that, my friends, is another story!

ABOUT ELIZABETH A. MILES

Photo courtesy of Angel Clausson/Tylerstar Productions

Author Elizabeth A. Miles is a certified life coach and founder of The Healing Connection, her coaching practice and growing online community where people can find support and encouragement as they move through their lives. She is also a speaker and the co-founder of the youth leadership series The Recipe for Leadership Project, designed to teach kids about communication, mindset, and taking leadership in their own lives. Liz obtained her bachelor's degree in psychology as well as her Master of Business Administration, and a diploma in baking and pastry. Elizabeth is a Philadelphia local, mom of four, animal lover, and loves reading, writing, and music. Connect with Elizabeth at www.healingconnection.us or find her on Facebook

(@HealingConnection.us) or Instagram (@healingconnection.us). #powertopivot